AMBERLEY CASTLE

1103 ~ 2003

Hunting Lodge, Fortified Manor, Country Castle Hotel

Best Wishes

Joy and Martin

FOLLOWING PAGES
Amberley Castle from the south.

David Arscott

Historical research by Annabelle Hughes

Amberley Castle

Hunting Lodge
Fortified Manor
Country Castle Hotel

First published in 2002 by The Dovecote Press Ltd
Stanbridge, Wimborne, Dorset BH21 4JD
on behalf of Amberley Castle
Amberley, Arundel, West Sussex BN18 9ND

ISBN 1 904349 04 8

Designed and produced by The Dovecote Press Ltd

Typeset in Monotype Sabon
Printed and bound by KHL Printing Co Pte Ltd, Singapore

A CIP catalogue record for this book is available
from the British Library

Contents

Foreword

BY MARTIN CUMMINGS

Amberley Castle is a gem, not flawless, but nevertheless very precious. Joy and I started with a pub, the Kings Arms Inn at Cookham-on-Thames, Berkshire, simply because we wished to work together. Its success encouraged us to take a step upwards to a small hotel at Godalming, Surrey, the Inn on the Lake. Buoyed by this further success, we went for the ultimate challenge in our industry – a country house hotel.

Originally a hunting lodge, then, successively a fortified manor, farm and a family home, Amberley Castle has, against all the odds, matured into one of the most respected and successful small luxury hotels in the world. Our trials and tribulations, which are given as a matter of fact in the final chapter, led us early on to believe that if something is worth having, it is worth fighting for! That has been our overwhelming experience. The silver lining has been friends, customers, staff and suppliers by their support and encouragement from the start.

From day one, our sales have never stopped increasing, to the point that a huge degree of pride exists amongst all those involved in the life of the castle. In turn, this has been a great source of strength to Joy and me, confirming our belief that our risks, sleepless nights and difficulties have been worthwhile.

The result is that although the magic, mystery and history are as poignant as ever, so too the castle's warmth, grandeur and homeliness sit happily side-by-side. 'Heaven on Earth' is one description given by a contented guest.

We have a passion for the place, which is obvious to all that meet us. People from all over the United Kingdom and, for that matter, the world, enjoy its peace and tranquillity so much that they return again and again. Some have 'popped the question', whilst many have married here, to say nothing of those who – for personal reasons – have been named after the castle.

Events today and in history are what Amberley Castle is made of. Our home and hotel is full of fond memories and has already played an important part in the minds of many. This book, which has been four years in the making, is the first serious project to reflect upon the 900 years of history that is Amberley Castle; we hope you enjoy reading it.

Martin and Joy Cummings in the Court Room at Amberley Castle with their Pyrenean mountain dogs Oban and Amber.

Introduction

A map shows little Amberley, its church and its castle tucked under the Sussex Downs in a bend of the River Arun, lapped by the plant-rich and bird-haunted waters of Amberley Wild Brooks and a good five miles from the nearest town. The newcomer might well believe, at least until the railway was laid across the neighbouring fields during the 1840s, that this was a spot remote from the hurly-burly of life – even though those castle defences betray the hint of a very different narrative.

If the map is a detailed one, however, any idea of a timeless slumber will be swiftly dispelled. High on the downs, behind the scar of the chalk pits, is an ancient 'field system', the remains of terraced fields, or lynchetts, first cultivated here some 6000 years ago. Within just a few Ordnance Survey squares, moreover, your eyes will alight upon a host of other prehistoric references: 'tumulus' (burial mound), 'enclosure', 'settlement' and (on Harrow Hill) 'flint mines'. There are ancient tracks everywhere, showing that the downs were a busy thoroughfare long before the Romans arrived to impose a new authority upon the countryside: their Stane Street (from London to Chichester) strikes like an arrow across the landscape just above Amberley, with the remains of a posting station two-and-a-half miles north at Hardham and one of the finest villas in Britain, with superb mosaic flooring, about three miles north-west at Bignor. At Fishbourne, near Chichester, are the remains of the largest Roman palace yet discovered west of the Alps. This was a busy, lived-in landscape.

When the Romans left around 410 AD and the first wave of land-hungry Saxons swarmed into Sussex (their chieftain Aelle landed near Selsey, some 16 miles south-west of Amberley), those local people who survived either fled or were forced to serve new masters. These newcomers so thoroughly occupied the country that practically all the names of our ancient Sussex villages and smaller landscape features

Amberley Castle from the Upper Court, with the medieval Great Room on the left.

A view of the castle's Lower
Court from the West Walls.

have Saxon origins: the word Amberley may derive from the personal
name Eanburh and 'ley', meaning meadow.

It was during the early Saxon period that Christianity took hold in
Sussex, and Amberley was to play a vital role both in its early success
and in its later development. St Wilfrid – the great northern bishop,
who built a monastery at Selsey – was granted some 10,000 acres of
land in south-west Sussex to help finance his missionary work, and
almost a quarter of this considerable estate was at Amberley. Churches
began to spread across the Sussex landscape.

Not that the Saxons themselves were to enjoy their new territory unopposed for very long. A mile or so downriver from Amberley, at Burpham, you can follow the ramparts of an impressive figure-of-eight fort – one of four major defences built in Sussex by Alfred the Great to keep marauding Vikings at bay during the ninth century. From the 860s these pirates came rampaging through coastal settlements and up river valleys, homing in on churches which provided them with valuable, easily-won loot: the community at Selsey was forced to take refuge in Chichester on more than one occasion. A Danish warrior, Canute, later became King of England, while the Normans – cousins of the Vikings, who had long since settled in France – were in turn to seize the English crown in 1066.

These events form the backdrop to our own story, which begins in 1103 and is similarly rich in incident. The English church, with a power almost to rival that of the king, set up its Sussex diocese at Chichester, and Bishop Luffa built a large, timber-framed open hall at Amberley to serve both as his hunting lodge and as an administrative centre for his local estate. This development marks the first phase of what we know today as Amberley Castle.

As we follow the highs and lows of this beautiful medieval survivor in its idyllic rural setting, we see English history passing before our eyes. At times the castle itself plays a role in that colourful pageant: its transformation into a fortified manor house reflected the disturbances of the fourteenth century, while in the sixteenth century it fell victim to the passions of Cromwell's followers in the Civil War. On other occasions (such as the heart-stopping flight of the future Charles II to the Sussex coast in search of a boat to take him to France) major events have swirled about it.

This is the story, then, not only of a remarkable building, but of the people who have lived and worked here and of the times they have known. As one of the popular newspapers used to boast of itself, 'all human life is here'.

David Arscott
Lewes, Sussex
OCTOBER 2002

The Conqueror's Sussex

Picture the scene on a fine summer's day in 1103 as an exceptionally tall man astride a sturdy horse leads a hunting party from his new timber-framed hall at Amberley. As the hounds surge yelping towards the river, our blonde giant perhaps casts a proprietorial eye upon the workmen busy chiselling stone on St Michael's church which is steadily rising next door.

This is Ralph Luffa, Bishop of Chichester and one of the Norman elite. Devout man of the cloth he may be, but he enjoys the trappings of real power. During the reign of William the Conqueror's son, William 'Rufus,' he demonstrated his toughness by threatening to resign in a potentially dangerous argument with the king over ecclesiastical privileges. Now the Conqueror's youngest son, Henry I, is on the throne, and the German-born Luffa is in his element. Although himself

OPPOSITE PAGE Chichester Cathedral. The powerful Norman bishops ruled their Sussex estates, including Amberley, from their base in Chichester.

BELOW A reconstruction of Bishop Luffa's timber-framed hunting lodge at Amberley.

THE UPPER GREENSAND

The rock on which the church and castle stand is a pale, yellowish sandstone, deposited some 100 million years ago when Sussex lay under a rising sea. Geologists regard the section around the castle as among the finest to be seen in the county. Sandstone was quarried from outcrops such as this to provide building stone, and a survey in the 1920s found that the castle stood 'not on the edge of a natural cliff, but on that of the pit from which it was digged'.

The soils of Sussex run in bands lying roughly east to west. This section shows Amberley Castle superimposed on a geological route from Brighton at the coast to Ashdown Forest in the north.

illiterate, Henry is wise enough to know not only that he needs educated men versed in Latin to run his state bureaucracy, but also that he needs to keep them content – the hunting concession on his estates at Amberley and Aldingbourne ('rights of free warren') is one of the perks Luffa has picked up along the way.

Amberley was ideally placed for the bishop's country retreat. Standing on a low ridge of upper greensand rock above the flood plain of the swift-flowing Arun, it was easily accessible from two headlands on the opposite, western bank: Bury, on a continuation of the same ridge, and Houghton, on chalk at the point a mile to the south where the river breaks through the downs on its way to the sea. These crossings gave the Chichester-based bishops access not only to their scattered estates on the east bank, but also to large areas of the northern part of their diocese and (via the winding track which first passed through Rackham, Parham Park and Cootham) to the port at Shoreham on the River Adur.

As bishop, Luffa inherited the simple timber-framed building erected on the site soon after the Conquest of 1066 (the land returned him a healthy income), but he had this converted into an impressive aisled hall which also served as a hunting lodge. Life was good!

For the Saxon inhabitants of the area, by contrast, life must have been at best uncertain. The Normans had seized their new kingdom with brutal thoroughness: how else could an army of some 12,000 men impose their will on an English population of one and a half million? They built great castles to guard each river-mouth, and Amberley folk would have been only too aware of the battlements a few miles

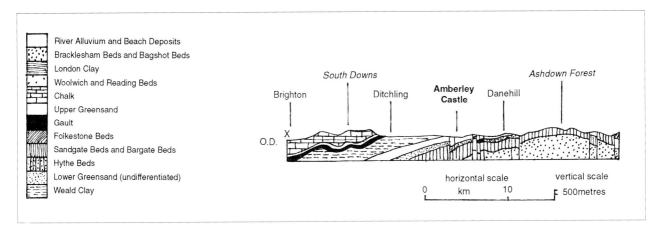

River Alluvium and Beach Deposits
Bracklesham Beds and Bagshot Beds
London Clay
Woolwich and Reading Beds
Chalk
Upper Greensand
Gault
Folkestone Beds
Sandgate Beds and Bargate Beds
Hythe Beds
Lower Greensand (undifferentiated)
Weald Clay

The Domesday Book entry for Amberley, 1086.

DOMESDAY

Amberley

Before 1066 and now it answered for 24 hides
Land for...In lordship 2 ploughs
20 villagers with 13 smallholders have 12 ploughs
Meadow 30 acres; woodland 7 pigs from pasturage
William the cleric holds 2 hides of this manor
Aldred the priest 3 hides; Baldwin 2½ hides
Ralph 2 hides less 1 virgate; Theodoric 3 hides; Guard 2 hides
Between them they have 3 ploughs in lordship and 17 villagers
and 25 small holders who have 5 ploughs
Value of the whole manor before 1066 £20; later £15;
now, what the Bishop holds £14;
Value of what the others hold from the Bishop £7

The Domesday Book entry for Amberley, 1086.

downstream at Arundel – built by Roger de Montgomery soon after the Conquest – frowning down upon the newly-subjugated people.

After the Battle of Hastings William's troops had marched west through Sussex, killing and destroying at will. When William sent his 'Domesday' commissioners throughout the land in 1086 to assess what every part of it was worth they discovered that, because of this devastation, many manors were worth far less than they had been twenty years earlier.

'There was not one single hide nor rood of land,' wrote the compilers of the *Anglo-Saxon Chronicle*, 'nor – it is shameful to tell, but he thought it no shame to do – was there an ox, cow or swine that was not set down in the writ.'

Amberley, belonging to the church, had not suffered the violence of some secular manors, although the Domesday record for this estate of nearly 3000 acres does show some falling off: 'Value of the whole manor before 1066 £20; later £15.' The bishop had a home farm of about 400 acres (ploughed by 33 tenants), with 30 acres of meadow and sufficient outlying woodland to support a herd of some 50 pigs. 'William the cleric' and 'Aldred the priest' – presumably Chichester cathedral clergy – were among a group of sub-tenants holding 300 acres

A Norman bishop.

THE MEDIEVAL HUNT

Hunting was regarded as an art as much as a sport in medieval times, when venison was an important part of the diet. The huntsmen used four main breeds of hound: the greyhound, the alaunt, the mastiff and the rache or running-hound. Several books were written about the technicalities and rituals involved. A good huntsman had to be able to shoot well with a bow, train his hounds to follow a trail, remember where the archers were placed, observe the wind, sound a horn correctly, make arrows and bow-strings, and skin and cut up a hart.

The Conqueror's oldest son, William Rufus, was killed by an arrow in the New Forest while out hunting – which is why his brother Henry was on the throne to grant Bishop Luffa his prized hunting rights.

worked by 42 of their own feudal underlings.

The feudal system imposed by the Normans was a pyramidal affair. The king was at the top, owning everything. His tenants-in-chief – the barons and prelates – held land from him direct, and they dispersed some of these holdings among a larger tier of lesser tenants, all bound together by mutual obligations, financial and military. Certainly the Bishop of Chichester would have been a rich and powerful man.

'In the medieval state,' the historian G.M. Trevelyan wrote, 'anarchy was a greater danger than despotism, though the opposite was the case in the medieval church.'

Luffa, doubtless loathed by many as a symbol of the harsh Norman yoke that now weighed them down, was nevertheless a caring and conscientious man, travelling around his diocese on preaching tours three times a year. On his travels he was well provided with resting places: at Amberley, where he had fashioned his new hunting lodge; at Cakeham, West Wittering, where there was probably also a timber-framed hall; and at Aldingbourne, where a moated castle site was the forerunner of the 'palace' which is known to lie to its east.

He was also a builder and beautifier of churches. The greatest of these was the cathedral at Chichester, begun soon after he became bishop in 1091, and built from greenish limestone dug from Quarr Abbey on the Isle of Wight. Luffa's patience and courage were both to be put to the test. After a great fire swept through the cathedral and the adjacent Bishop's Palace in 1114, he requested tax exemptions on the land and building materials to help towards the rebuilding – and twisted Henry I's arm by shutting up his parish churches, barricading the doors behind thorns and forbidding all services until he relented. The cathedral, growing gradually, would not be consecrated until 1184, some 60 years after his death.

Luffa was almost certainly responsible for rebuilding the wooden church at Amberley in stone. Perhaps the masons he brought from France to grace the cathedral with their skills worked here, too, creating those early features of the building which can still be made out among later additions. The settlement itself would have been no more than a hamlet of humble cottages at this time, the church appearing all the grander for its air of majestic permanence.

We shall never know whether Luffa intended to give his adjacent hunting lodge a similar treatment. In the event his successor, the

aristocratic and controversial Seffrid I (1124-47), was to create the first durable building on the site, using rubble masonry to build an 'open hall' here. Perhaps he, too, brought workmen over from Chichester, since a splendid chancel screen in Caen stone at the cathedral dates from the same period.

Seffrid, formerly Abbot of Glastonbury and a half brother to the Archbishop of Canterbury, was given the nickname 'Pelochin' (after a Bulgarian heretic), possibly hinting at dubious money dealing, but his expulsion from the see in mysterious circumstances probably had a political motive, because he was a known confidant of King Stephen's powerful and untrustworthy brother Henry, Bishop of Winchester.

A generation later Seffrid II (1180-1204) – possibly a young relative of his namesake – created a two-storey range of buildings to provide more suitable private accommodation together with service rooms and storage. His was a T-shaped building, the long cross-stroke of the T (now known as the east wing) lying roughly north-south against the churchyard, and the stubby down-stroke forming the range which now contains the present Great Room and Queens' Room – although there was then no separation between the floors.

Seffrid's building work at Amberley also coincided with renovations

RESTLESS REBUILDING

By comparing the remains at Amberley with the ways in which other buildings have developed, a broad sequence of the castle's early days can be set out:

• A timber-framed estate building, c. 1066.

• A timber-framed, aisled open hall built for a hunting lodge by Bishop Luffa, about 1103.

• An open hall in stone to replace the timber-framed hall, probably built by Luffa's successor Seffrid I (1124-47), followed quickly by

• A stone two-storey range built at right angles to provide more suitable private accommodation as well as service rooms and storage, probably by Seffrid II (1180-1204).

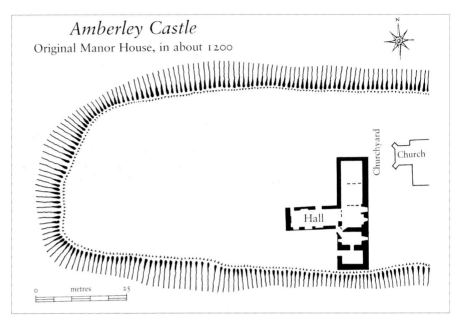

Amberley Castle
Original Manor House, in about 1200

An artist's idea of how the manor house might have looked after John of Langton had added the Great Hall in the early fourteenth century. The original open hall built by Seffrid I was probably converted into the chapel.

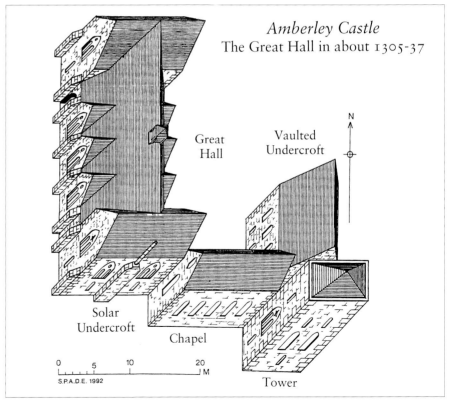

Amberley Castle
The Great Hall in about 1305-37

S.P.A.D.E. 1992

at Chichester, this time of a more profound nature. On October 20, 1187, three years after Seffrid had consecrated it, the cathedral was ravaged by another disastrous fire. The work was sufficiently complete to allow re-consecration in 1199, the year in which Seffrid took part in the coronation of King John (of Magna Carta fame). He established the St James' Hospital for Lepers in Chichester and is buried in the Lady Chapel of the cathedral.

Ralph Neville (1224-45) was another bishop who must have come to know Amberley well, since he rebuilt the chancel of the parish church, which at this time served as his chapel. (Towards the end of the century a later bishop, no doubt seeking more privacy, built a chapel somewhere in the south-west of the castle grounds.) All bishops were men of standing, but this one was also Henry III's chancellor of the realm. Surviving correspondence between Neville and his steward, Simon de Seinliz, reveals that Amberley and his other Sussex estates provided a regular supply of wool, beef, venison and horses to the bishop's London residence, as well as returning profits from a wide range of produce and, when required, making a good impression on those even more powerful than the bishop: 'If you please, I will pay attention to [the Lord Archbishop of Canterbury] so that it shall turn to your advantage and honour; and you may know for certain that as long as he has sojourned at Slindon [five miles south-west of Amberley], attention was paid to him in presents from your manors of Aldingeburne and Amberley.'

The manor, or estate, was one of the earliest administrative divisions in England, even older than the parish. The land of a manor did not all have to be in the same place, and sometimes included distant pieces of woodland or pasture. 'Demesne' land was the lord's home farm, as distinct from the lands of the villeins and sub-tenancies, and it was generally exempt from taxation.

Manorial services were onerous, and life was hard for tenants and their families in feudal times. Apart from looking after their own land-holding, they had to carry out a range of duties for the lord of the manor. Working in his woods or in his portion of the great open fields that gave medieval England its character would have been the greatest of these, but they might also be called upon to assist the brewer, to look after the draught oxen and horses, to fold his flocks over the nearby downs, to work local ferries or to carry produce and firewood to the

distant parts of his far-flung manor. The tenant was responsible for seeing that his work for the lord was performed, using as many members of his family as he could muster, or pay an equivalent sum of money in lieu. Regular courts were held, with fines for those who failed to attend, and when a man died, his best (or only) animal had to be given to the lord as death duty. The bishop would certainly not always be held in high regard by his Amberley tenants.

Where Neville was worldly, his successor was saintly – and, indeed, was later canonised. Richard de Wych (1245-53), one of the earliest

Two views of St Richard's Gate, leading from the castle grounds into St Michael's churchyard. The engraving was made in 1807.

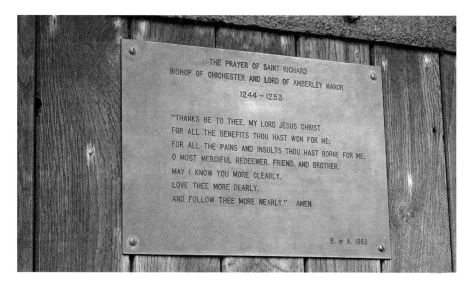

A version of St Richard's prayer is affixed to the gate at Amberley which bears his name.

recorded doctors of canon law at Oxford, was chancellor to the university in the 1230s, and became chancellor to the Archbishop of Canterbury around 1237. Despite these impressive credentials, Henry III at first refused to accept his appointment to Chichester. With royal men-at-arms preventing him even from entering the city, he lodged with the rector of Tarring, near Worthing, ministering to the poor in their hovels. When, after two years, the king gave way, Richard was at last able to visit his estates (records show that he visited Amberley at least twice) and he immediately set about religious and administrative reforms. Wearing a hairshirt and iron bands about his body, he won a reputation for performing miracles.

Ten years after his death in 1252, while preaching a crusade, he was declared a saint, and his tomb in Chichester Cathedral became a shrine for pilgrimages. His detailed will survives and includes bequests to many ordinary people, including the nephew of Simon, the rector of Tarring, a former cook and 'the boys who have waited on me'.

Of course, both the spiritual and the temporal were a bishop's concern on his estates. A record of 1279 shows a wide range of livestock at Amberley: three horses, 20 oxen (for ploughing), a bull and 20 cows, six rams and 400 sheep, a boar and four breeding sows as well as about 40 pigs for slaughter, a gander and 32 geese, and 54 chickens, including a cock. In addition, nearly 200 hens and 950 eggs were collected each year as rent.

Hunting, as ever, was a major attraction for the sportsman. From the time that Bishop Luffa built his hunting lodge, Amberley had claimed sole rights to hunting at neighbouring Houghton, but in 1280 Bishop Stephen fell out with the Arundel estate about the boundaries of the chase. The argument rumbled on for years, the dispute coming to a head in 1292 when his successor, Bishop Gilbert, not only accused Richard Fitzalan, the lord of Arundel Castle, of hunting there illegally, but took the extreme step of publicly excommunicating him.

The feelings aroused can best be judged by reading a later entry in the bishop's register about illegal hunting on his estate at Selsey: 'Certain sons of damnation . . . seduced by a devilish spirit and abandoning the fear of God, hunted in our park at Selsey with hounds, nets and arrows and other instruments . . . broke down the fences of the park and dared to chase, slay and carry away deer and other wild animals therein; all and singular such persons are adjudged to have incurred the greater excommunication to be pronounced them in every church in the deanery with upraised cross, bells ringing and candles lighted.'

So it was to be for Fitzalan who, having at first shrugged his shoulders, found that the punishment had been extended to his whole estate – doubtless to the horror of his many God-fearing tenants. Excommunication cut them off from all the sacraments and services of the Church – no light matter at a time when religion was an inextricable part of daily life.

There can be few better demonstrations of the extraordinary power the church had over men's souls than the humiliating journey the earl was forced to make on Christmas Eve, riding up from Arundel to meet Gilbert at Houghton chapel to receive absolution so that he and his household could celebrate the festival as the church expected.

And what if the earl had resisted? John of Langton (1305-37), one of the lesser known bishops of Chichester, had risen from being a humble clerk in chancery (or civil servant) to the heady post of Chancellor under both Edward I and Edward II, and he played a key role in the dangerous political turmoils of the period. This no doubt hardened him for his later confrontation with Earl John de Warenne (descendant of one of the Conqueror's chief nobles, the builder of Lewes Castle), whom he excommunicated for adultery. De Warenne, rather than submit as Fitzalan had done, threatened John with violence – whereupon the bishop had the earl and his followers imprisoned.

FORM OF WORDS FOR GREATER EXCOMMUNICATION

'By the authority of God the Father, Son and Holy Ghost, Mary the Blessed Mother of God and all the saints, we excommunicate, anathematize and cut off from the privileges of Holy Church those malefactors, their aiders and abettors, and unless they repent and offer satisfaction may their candle be put out before the living God for ever and ever. So be it, Amen.'

A lighted candle was then dashed out on the pavement of the church.

This doughty character, who built the chapter house and possibly parts of the palace at Chichester, is also thought to have been responsible for the castle's Great Hall, with its associated solar and service rooms, whose ruins remain in the grounds to this day. Whenever the bishop was staying at Amberley with his retinue, the reeve and half a dozen other tenants were invited to eat in the hall with the household servants. Every three weeks the estate 'hallmote', or court, would be held in the hall, and the vicar was expected to find a scribe to write the minutes and to keep the records and rent lists up to date.

Such duties apart, here was a retreat from the hustle and bustle of life in Chichester or London, where a seasoned public servant could for the most part put his feet up and relax. The bishop was now, we may assume, staying here on a regular basis, rather than simply regarding the estate as a useful source of income.

If God was in his heaven, however, all was not right with the world.

The ruins of the Great Hall. It was here that the business of the Amberley estates was conducted, with regular meetings of the bishop, his reeve and the most influential tenants, to fix rents and decide disputes of various kinds.

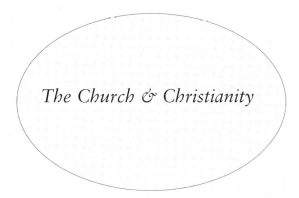

The Church & Christianity

Amberley and its neighbouring villages have a special place in the early spread of Christianity in Sussex, because they were among the 10,000 acres of land given to Bishop Wilfrid of Northumbria to support his missionary work soon after he arrived here in 680.

Wilfrid was a learned, highly impressive but cantankerous character who fell out with a succession of kings and archbishops, not least over the burning issue of whether the English church should adopt the Celtic or the Roman rites – having studied (and made his mark) in Rome, he supported the latter. He landed in Sussex while exiled from his home kingdom, eventually staying for several years to build a monastery at Selsey and

---

AD 683

Grant by Caedwalla, king of Wessex, to Bishop Wilfrid of land at Selsey &c

In the name of our Saviour Jesus Christ! We have brought nothing into this world and it is certain we can carry nothing out. Therefore the eternal and heavenly rewards of the Kingdom on high are to be sought instead of earthly and transitory things.

On that account, I Caedwalla, king by the grace of God, have been asked by the venerable Bishop Wilfrid to be so good as to grant him a little land for the support of the followers of Christ who lead a monastic life, and for the construction of a monastery on the place which is called Selsey. In addition I will give in his own power of gift the land which is called Aldingbourne and Lidsey, of 6 hides; and 6 at Westergate, and 8 at Mundham, and 8 at Amberley and Houghton, and 4 at Coldwaltham, that is 32 hides.

This charter was written in the year of our Lord's Incarnation 683, on the 3rd day of the month of August.

The charter of 683 – probably forged – showing the grant of land, including Amberley, by King Caedwalla to Wilfrid.

begin to organise the structure of the church.

None of the stories of Wilfrid's exploits is entirely trustworthy. The Venerable Bede, the first chronicler of the English, tells us that he taught the locals how to catch fish by using nets – a highly unlikely tale from an author who also claims that at times of drought and famine these same people were in the habit of leaping lemming-like to their deaths from clifftops (at Beachy Head, perhaps?) rather than suffer a lingering death.

Even the charter which records the transfer of land to Wilfrid is doubtful. It was almost certainly a gift from King Aethelwealh, who had married a Christian wife, been baptised with his nobles in Mercia, brought priests back to baptise his people and allowed a small band of Irish monks to settle at Bosham, on the edge of Chichester Harbour. The charter, dated 683, purports to show that it was King Caedwalla who granted the land, but this was almost certainly a later forgery intended to bolster the Church's claim to it: Caedwalla, who invaded Sussex in 685 and killed Aethelwealh, has been described as 'a pagan thug from Wessex' and seems a most unlikely donor.

On receiving his new estates, Wilfrid immediately freed the 250 slaves who were attached to them – presumably the descendants of

The modern stained glass memorial window to St Wilfrid in Ripon Cathedral. At the bottom right he is seen in a boat, teaching the men of Selsey to fish.

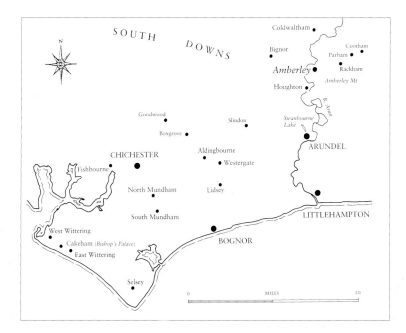

LEFT A map showing locations around Amberley mentioned in the text, including the estates granted to Wilfrid by the king.

BELOW Surviving medieval wall paintings are few and far between in Sussex churches, but Amberley has several fragments. The largest is to the right of the chancel arch, and includes a depiction of Christ in Majesty, with the world between his feet and his right hand raised in blessing.

RIGHT The churchyard at Amberley is managed to allow wild flowers to flourish. The east wing of the castle can be seen beyond the wall.

Britons overrun by the Saxon advance two hundred years earlier. His monastery at low-lying Selsey was reached by a causeway, and he must have been fondly reminded of his youth as a novice with the monks on the island of Lindisfarne.

When Wilfrid left in 686, the church in Sussex was still controlled from Wessex, but in 705 the county was given its own home-grown bishop, and Wilfrid's monastery became his headquarters. New churches now began to rise in the landscape. Made of timber, they have all since disappeared (some of them, almost certainly, fired by the Viking raiders who tormented Sussex during the ninth and tenth centuries), but a great many of our early stone churches, including St Michael's at Amberley, stand on those same sites today – a continuity of some 1300 years.

It was the Normans who transferred the administrative centre of the bishopric to Chichester in 1075, for a number of reasons: it was a thriving urban centre with a royal mint; most of the bishopric's estates were in the area; there was already a minster church on the site where Ralph Luffa would soon build his cathedral; and the Selsey site was, in any case, threatened by the rising sea.

Now the church would grow in wealth and influence, and the bishops would expand and embellish their estate at Amberley first granted to Bishop Wilfrid.

Troubled Times

The barges, heavily laden with stone and timber, nose their way up the Arun, making for the landing place closest to the curtain walls steadily rising from the watery flatlands close to the river. It is the summer of 1381, and Bishop William Reede, watching the builders completing their work on his new castle, turns to greet a messenger hotfoot from the cathedral with alarming news: Wat Tyler and his rebels are at the gates of London. They have murdered the archbishop. 'Just in time,' breathes Reede, resting his hand on the stout stone wall. 'Just in time!'

This is an imagined scene, but entirely plausible. Reede, appointed bishop in 1370, must have envied the confidence with which John of Langton had built the Great Hall at Amberley only a generation earlier. So much had changed since then – and changed for the worse.

First, the French wars. The incessant battles and skirmishes which were to become known as the Hundred Years War had begun in 1337 and were to last until 1453. To pay for them, Edward III and now Richard II ('the boy king') had imposed a succession of hated poll taxes on the people, leading to widespread unrest.

Next, and more terrible by far, the Black Death had stolen ashore at a southern port and, during the spring of 1349, had begun to cut a swathe through the population of Sussex, dooming countless thousands to an agonising death. A third, perhaps a half, of the population perished, and the survivors inhabited a new world in which the old certainties, the old feudal order, had gone for ever. In an unkempt landscape where fields lay untilled for want of labour, the centuries-old system of exact duties owed by each tenant to his lord could not long survive. Labour had a new value, and many of those who offered themselves for hire lacked the old subservience. There was a spirit of bloody-mindedness in the air.

The mighty gatehouse of Amberley Castle, with its battlements and sturdy portcullis beyond the moat. The castle was strengthened at a time of French wars and civil unrest.

The Latin original of the '*licenti crenellandi*', or 'licence to crenellate'.

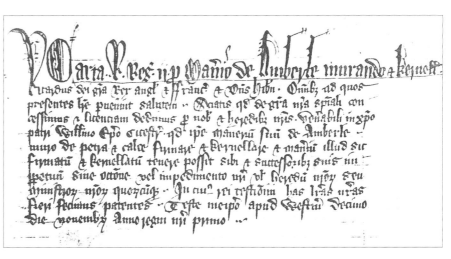

'Charter roll of the King for the Manor of Amberle for fortifying and crenellating.

Richard, by the grace of God, King of England and France and Lord of Ireland; to all whom these present letters shall come, greetings. Know that we, of our special grace have granted and given a licence for our own part and on behalf of our heirs, to our venerable father in Christ, William, Bishop of Chichester, that he may fortify and crenellate his manor of Amberle with walls of stone and lime, and he and his successors may hold his said manor so fortified and crenellated forever without interference or impediment from us or our heirs or any of our ministers. In testimony of which we have made these letters patent. Given under my own witness at Westminster, 10 November in the first year of our reign.

It was against this background of potential civil unrest that on November 10, 1377 Richard II granted Bishop Reede a 'licence to crenellate', or build battlements, at Amberley. Kings raised cash through such licences, which they would issue to men who posed no perceptible threat to them, and they were also providing for themselves a series of 'safe houses' to use on their travels. We have no record of the

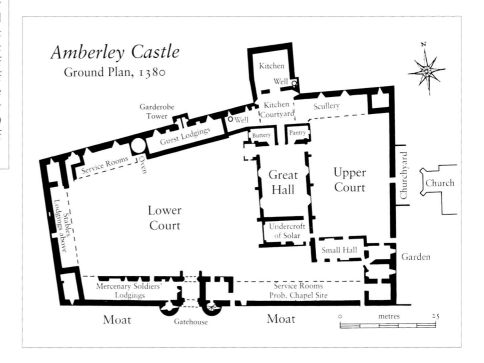

reason Reede officially advanced for needing one, but perhaps it was similar to that given by Sir Edward Dalyngrigge at Bodiam, in the far east of the county, only a few years later: 'To strengthen with a wall of stone and lime, and crenellate and construct and make into a castle his manor-house of Bodyham, near the sea, in the county of Sussex, for defence of the adjacent country and resistance to our enemies.'

Amberley was intended to be impregnable, too, its lofty curtain walls up to 60 feet high built with Caen stone from northern France: (the quarries can still be seen today, and house the French War Museum). The masons were highly skilled men, their arts passed down the generations from those who had fashioned strongholds in the Savoy region of France and, in turn, erected the chain of sturdy castles along the English border with Wales.

A moat ran along its southern side, the marshes of the Wild Brooks shielded it to the north and the small postern, or water-gate, which survives in the west wall suggests that there was some natural protection from that side, too. Some of its features, however, indicate that the bishop was not anticipating pitched battles with invading armies. The towers at each corner, for instance, projected internally and would therefore have been unable to provide flanking fire along the east and west walls. The twin-towered gatehouse had a drawbridge and portcullis, but it lacked the machicolations which were at that time commonplace – overhanging parapets supported on corbels above the gateway, with openings for discharging missiles on assailants below.

Although French raids up the River Arun were certainly a possibility, the suspicion must be that Bishop Reede's worries lay closer to home. After all, Arundel Castle was far better equipped to deal with a military assault than Amberley, and it lay somewhat closer to the coast. The threat to a rich and powerful prelate was more likely to come from disaffected members of the local community, dismayed by a run of poor harvests and enraged by the efforts of landlords to reinforce the control of labour on their estates. Reede doubtless recalled that the Bishop of Exeter had been murdered outside his London residence back in 1327, prompting at least two princes of the Church to apply for licences to fortify their palaces. Now, fifty years on, even sleepy Sussex seemed threatened by the lawlessness of a disaffected peasantry.

Between 1376 and 1378 there were rural demonstrations against landlords in some forty villages from Sussex to Devon, and Amberley

BISHOP REEDE (1370-1385)

William Reede, consecrated as a bishop at Avignon, was a true academic – a Doctor of Law from Merton College, Oxford, with a reputation as a mathematician.

His will, in which he left money for the continuing work at the castle, reveals a great deal about his interests and priorities. He made numerous bequests to Sussex churches and priories, and a chalice on display in the British Museum may be the one he left to Rusper Priory, where it was discovered during excavations in the late 1800s.

Bishop Reede bequeathed astronomical instruments to Merton College and a hundred pounds in gold and money for the repair of the library at Exeter College. Although he wished to be buried at Selsey, as the original site of the diocese, his final resting place was Chichester Cathedral.

Amberley Castle, 1380

A reconstruction by John Hodgson of Amberley Castle from the south in about 1380, showing it with the 'crenellations', or battlements, constructed by Bishop Reede.

On the right is the bishop's potager, or herb garden, and the gateway into the churchyard. To the left of the garden is the Great Hall, with the solar at the southern end.

The long building at the back of the courtyard is the bishop's guesthouse, complete with its chimneys and garderobe tower. Squeezed between the guesthouse and half-timbered storeroom is the bread oven, and on the left are the stables.

We know from Bishop Reede's will that the building work was unfinished on his death in 1385, hence the piles of timber and building materials in the courtyard.

JOHN
HODGSON

Castle's existing walls would have been inadequate to keep out an organised military force. Amberley was the only one of the bishop's country manors that was cheek-by-jowl with the local community, and 'security fencing' was essential to separate the castle from the village, both visibly and socially. Two of the bishop's properties in the east of the county – Michelham Priory (where a sturdy stone gatehouse was erected over the moat) and Wilmington Priory – were fortified at about the same time and, one suspects, for the same reason.

Rebellion broke out after the imposition of a third poll tax in three years to finance foreign wars. There was universal evasion, and the government's attempts to collect unpaid taxes triggered off the spontaneous peasant risings in Sussex and Kent which culminated in Wat Tyler's march on London in June, 1381. The mob occupied the City, sacked the palace of John of Gaunt, the Temple and Clerkenwell Priory, released prisoners from the gaols and killed the Archbishop of Canterbury and the Prior of the Order of St John of Jerusalem. They made demands for the abolition of serfdom and rent controls, and forced concessions from the young Richard II – promises which were later broken.

Reede, his fears justified, continued to build at Amberley Castle.

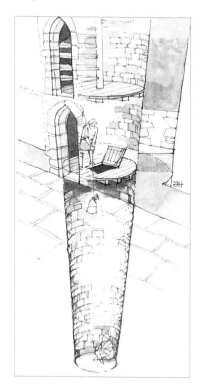

Bishops were entitled to have their own lock-ups, and it is hardly surprising that he seems to have installed an oubliette, a deep underground cell covered by a heavy iron grille where any poor devil might well imagine himself (as the name terribly implies) completely forgotten. Was this the place where some years later (1415) William Fretton, a clerk from Coombes, near Steyning, was incarcerated under the eye of the gaoler, John Chilting, for committing a felony?

Many of the changes, however, were domestic. Bishop Reede enlarged the manor's capacity for lodging household staff, with a new Great Hall, a buttery and pantry, separate apartments for guests and retainers and a suite of rooms along the north and south curtain walls: although these have gone, the fireplaces, joist holes and corbels for roof supports can still be seen today. The magnificent garderobes ('two of the finest latrines to have survived from the Middle Ages,' enthuses John Guy in his book *Castles of Sussex*) discharged into water below the north wall: the shafts can be seen from outside the wall as arches thrown across the external angles of the tower.

The bishop also built a new kitchen, projecting beyond the walls as a

Days of sail. A barge on the River Arun during the late nineteenth century, with the village of Bury in the background.

fire precaution – further evidence for the theory that military fortification was hardly uppermost in his mind – and he converted the hall range of the original manor house into his chapel by taking out the hall floor and putting in a tall south window.

The fortifications had not been completed when Reede died, but his will ensured that the work would continue after his death: 'I leave on behalf of works of stone and wood in the manors of Amberle and Aldynbourne begun by me, fifty marks . . . my successor to let my executor have stones, sand, chalk, wood in the chase at Houghton . . . together with the bishop's barges for the carriage . . . and sufficient timber for every work of wood.'

Bishop Reede's register has survived, and it gives a good picture of the business he and later bishops carried out when they stayed at Amberley. However much they used their country residence to relax, their 'office' came with them, and they had to hear petitions, make appointments and pronounce excommunications. The register shows that the bishop sent out notices of his inspections of parish clergy and orders of monks and nuns; confirmed the appointments of priests to parishes; issued instructions to senior clergy about supervising the behaviour of the lower clergy and parishioners; responded to royal pronouncements; heard cases regarding illegitimacy; and made grants of funds or indulgences to deserving individuals.

The brand new castle at Amberley was on those occasions the very seat of ecclesiastical government in Sussex. In 1397, for instance, the newly-elected abbot of Robertsbridge, Dom William Lewes, arrived in 'the great chamber of the Manor of Amberle' to ask for the Bishop's approval. The bishop's blessing was given 'at the hour of Mattins in his Chapel there', and the abbot distributed 23s 4d among the officials present.

Various records survive from the medieval period to give us an idea of day-to-day life at Amberley. Until Bishop Praty built a stone bridge across the river at Houghton in 1450, travellers from the south and west had either to use an old clapper bridge of planks slung across stone plinths (not, one imagines, a dignified approach) or to take a ferry. Fourteenth century documents frequently record the feudal obligation to carry goods and people across the river: 'Geoffrey Blaunchard . . . shall help ferrying the lord and his household when he comes to Amberle and when he goes. When the lord comes he shall have his dinner one day, but not when he goes unless he ferries him after dinner.'

The bishop's arable land at Amberley was valued relatively poorly

A FAITHFUL SERVANT

The bishop had a steward at Amberley to keep an eye on the staff in residence and to look after the day-to-day organisation and maintenance of his house, particularly when he was away. This was a responsible job, and these men could be well-to-do in their own right. George Rose, a steward who died in 1530, left specific instructions about his burial:

'My body to be buried in the parish church of St Michael of Amberley by the north door . . . I will there be made in the north door a Tomb ceiled and painted with a crucifix and my picture with my two children therein and I give two images to be set in the said Tomb.'

Rose, who came from Nottinghamshire, also left rosaries to the bishop's chaplains and servants, but his elaborate tomb must have fallen foul of Puritan zeal in the following century, for no trace remains.

A ferry operated from Bury across the river to Amberley until well into the twentieth century.

GHOSTLY EMILY

Every castle seems to have its ghost, and Amberley is no exception. Several visitors have been aware of a 'presence', described as peaceful and unfrightening, in one of the rooms of the tower house, by the castle entrance.

This is Emily, a humble serving girl said to have been seduced and made pregnant by one of the bishops: the story goes that the body of a mother and her child were found close to the vicarage in unconsecrated ground. Cast aside, Emily climbed the staircase through the Herstmonceux Room and, in grief and despair, threw herself from the battlements.

Visitors have reported seeing cushions move, and finding locked doors mysteriously unlocked.

during the 13th and 14th centuries because it was broken up into strips and intermingled with the fields of his tenants in the old common field system. The income from his fields and meadows, woodland and sheep runs was, nonetheless, considerable. As farmers continued to clear the forests of the weald and take their ploughs further up the downland slopes, they grew wheat, barley, oats, beans, pot-herbs and vetches (for animal forage), while the widespread practice of settling feudal dues by an Easter 'gift' of eggs or hens to the lord of the manor is recorded in Bishop Reede's 'rental': 'John de la Stokke holds a croft . . . He shall give 5 eggs at Easter' and 'William Pulayn and William Ailmer render 2 hens and 20 eggs at Easter'.

There are clues in the rental to the style of life the bishop would have enjoyed while staying at Amberley. Some of the serfs took it in turns to act as reeve – the officer in charge of local administration and deciding disputes. The chosen man would pay no rent during the period, and 'if he is delayed till after nones [about 3pm] he shall then have his dinner of the lord. He shall be at the lord's table from Lammas to Michelmas after nones, and shall have his food as long as the Bishop is in the township, and likewise when the steward is there in the lord's court.'

And the castle had to be kept clean, of course. Emma, a householder, seems to have been given what we would call a tied cottage for her labours. She 'shall clean out the Hall and the lord's chambers against his arrival, and as often as is needed while he is in the township. She shall gather 2 bundles of rushes to strew in the rooms.'

Life, then, was for the most part busy but uneventful – but the troubles had not gone away. Public unrest came to a head again in the summer of 1450 when Sussex men in their hundreds deserted their towns and villages to join Jack Cade's rebellion against the corruptions of Henry VI's government. This was not mob rule: the lists of those involved included labourers, craftsmen and tradesmen, yeomen farmers, the clerks of Dallington and Wartling, the chaplain of Mayfield and even the prior of St Pancras at Lewes with all his men and servants.

Similarities with the Peasants' Revolt of 1381 are striking. Cade's army, like Tyler's, stormed the capital, failing only to take the Tower of London. Two of the most hated men in the kingdom – one of them the Lord Treasurer, Sir James Fiennes, younger brother of the man who built Herstmonceux Castle in East Sussex – had their heads severed and stuck on poles, where they were made to exchange a ghastly kiss. And once again concessions were granted, only to be snatched away when the danger had passed.

And the Bishop of Chichester, Adam Moleyns? Perhaps he should have sought the shelter of his fortified Amberley retreat, but it appears that he decided to scuttle. He was seized as he was about to board a ship at Portsmouth, and summarily killed by the sailors. The remnants of the defensive earthworks he had only recently thrown up at his manor at Bexhill can still be seen today. Moleyns, one of Henry's favourites, had been given permission to crenellate the manor – but in his case it was too late.

A traditional wooden clapper bridge spanned the Arun at Houghton until the bishop ordered a more substantial stone bridge to be built here in 1450.

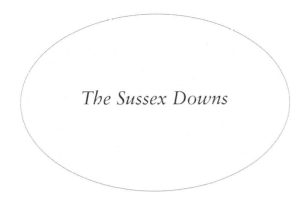

The Sussex Downs

They rise above the castle to a height of some 500ft at the proud promontory of Amberley Mount, those rolling hills up to six miles wide which Rudyard Kipling called 'our blunt, bow-headed, whale-backed Downs' and which for the naturalist Gilbert White were 'that chain of majestic mountains'. Running west from the white cliffs of Beachy Head and the Seven Sisters across the breadth of the county into Hampshire, they are to many – natives and visitors alike – a symbol of Sussex itself. In days gone by, less wooded than the clay country of the Weald below, they provided safe routes for pilgrims and other travellers on their way from Canterbury to Chichester, Winchester and beyond. Today, soon to be designated a National Park, they offer a peaceful retreat from the clamour of life at their foot.

A massive, scarcely imaginable subterranean collision of tectonic plates millions of years ago buckled the earth's crust, threw up the mountain ranges of the Himalayas and the Alps and – by a ripple effect – twisted and fractured the landscape of Sussex. Over millions more years the great chalk dome which covered this 'wealden anticline' was eroded by rivers, seas and the elements, bequeathing us the varied and beautiful landscape we see today. To the south the Sussex Downs slope gently towards the sea, while to the north (as above Amberley) they are much steeper and, because more shaded and damp, support a different range of wildlife.

Largely bare of trees in the east of the county, the downs are more wooded the further west you go, with great stands of beech – their leaves burning vividly in autumnal sunlight – growing on the deposits known as clay-with-flints. Some patches of woodland in the western downs, moreover, are rare survivals of the uncleared ancient wildwood, their typical plants being lichens, lily of the valley and dog's mercury.

The downland sward is one of the richest habitats in western Europe. The home of the brown hare and the rabbit, this is a landscape alive with bees and grasshoppers, glow-worms, chalk-loving snails and a wide range of butterflies – the blues on the warmer slopes, the dark green fritillary and marbled white in the coarse grasses of the northern escarpment.

ABOVE A view of the Downs above Upwaltham, looking towards Dog Kennel Cottages.

RIGHT Sheep grazing in the snow near Amberley Mount. Before the last war sheep covered the downs in their tens of thousands, manuring the soil and cropping the turf.

OPPOSITE PAGE Bee orchid.

ABOVE LEFT Marbled white butterfly. LEFT Common blue butterfly.

ABOVE The chalkpit by Amberley station in about 1910. A cart loaded with chalk is harnessed to a working horse before being pulled to one of the limekilns. A thriving business operated here from the 1840s until the 1960s.

OPPOSITE PAGE A field of poppies on the downland slopes above Sutton.

Only about five per cent of prime grassland has survived the ravages of plough, property developer and encroaching scrub, but here you will find as many as forty species of plant within a square metre. The thin rendzina soil is rich in calcium but low in vital plant nutrients such as nitrates, phosphates and iron, which sink into the porous chalk almost without trace, and the great survivors are chiefly small, slow-growing plants which individually take little space: violets, cowslips, harebells, orchids and a host of sweet-scented herbs. Until the Second World War the constant nibbling by huge flocks of sheep prevented grasses, thistles and the like from shading out the smaller plants. Now, however, most of the sheep have gone and the remaining high-quality habitat is threatened.

The sheep once played an important part in manuring the poor chalk soil of the downs, but agricultural lime was also in great demand by farmers. Close to Houghton Bridge, and now the home of a fine industrial museum, is a large chalkpit which was worked from at least 1841 until the 1960s, its kilns producing lime both for farmers and for the building trade. A canal cut from the River Arun was constructed in the early years. At its peak the pit employed more than a hundred men, and a large stable of working horses to haul loads of chalk to the mouths of the kilns. The chalk was then burned, using layers of faggots, wood and coal. The lime burners were the elite of the workforce, each responsible for his own kiln and producing some six tons a day.

he excellētor renesmop is to magnif

Tudor Glories

As the last of the gorgeously painted oak panels is fixed to the wall, Bishop Robert Sherborne makes a tour of inspection, pausing with satisfaction before each sumptuous portrait. All represent women of antiquity dressed as for some impossibly fashionable Renaissance pageant – tight-fitting velvet, damask and jewelled costumes beneath highly decorated armour hung with tiny bells. Each (Cassandra and Semiramis, Sinope and Thamoris) carries a heraldic shield and a weapon or symbol of her identity. Sherborne, one of Chichester's most cultured bishops, knows how to interpret the coded language of each picture. Will King Henry perhaps come here to Amberley to share his pleasure?

The celebrated Amberley Panels, representations by the artist Lambert Bernard of what have variously been called 'queens', 'virtuous women' and 'sybils', mark a high point in the fortunes of Amberley Castle and of the bishops who made it their home-from-home. Bernard's glowing use of colour, and the richness of gold leaf and silver in the painted room, would have left a visitor to the castle in no doubt as to the status and power of its owner.

Sherborne was Bishop of Chichester from 1508 until 1536, and so witnessed both the glorious pomp and the dangerous political and religious confrontations of Henry VIII's turbulent reign. 'King Hal' came to the throne in 1509 as a gilded youth, fiercely intelligent, a prodigious athlete and accomplished in the arts. His father had ended the bloody Wars of the Roses in 1485 by defeating Richard III at the Battle of Bosworth Field, so installing on the throne the great Tudor line: the red rose of Lancaster had finally overcome the white rose of York. When Henry became king, he gathered about him the leading scholars of his day (Erasmus, John Colet, Sir Thomas More), so encouraging the spread of the New Learning based on ancient texts and art.

Roses in the Amberley Castle gardens are a reminder of the bitter strife between the houses of Lancaster and York in the 15th century. The top photograph is of the Lancastrian red of *Rosa gallica* 'officinalis', whilst below it is the Yorkist white of *Rosa alba* 'maxima'.

OPPOSITE PAGE Queen Sinope, one of the richly painted Amberley Panels.

The Queens' Room, 1840.

A diplomat and scholar, and very much a man of the English Renaissance, Bishop Sherborne must have relished these early years under his charismatic young monarch. The bishop himself used art and architecture at least in part as a form of self-promotion, enriching and repairing his run-down palaces at Chichester and Cakeham (on the coast, near the mouth of Chichester harbour), and modernising Amberley, his favourite residence, by putting a first floor into the small hall – so creating the splendid Queens' Room with its barrel-vaulted ceiling. In an age of brick chimneys with outside flues, the days of vast draughty and smoky open halls were numbered: Amberley was an early example of a more cosy and, above all, gracious way of living.

Bishop Sherborne.

Bernard was, in effect, Sherborne's 'court painter'. He may have been French or Flemish by birth, but his use of distemper on plaster and wood, rather than the more usual oil painting, was peculiarly English. Sherborne employed him for many years, and his work can be seen in the cathedral (including two huge propaganda 'history' paintings and a series of medallion portraits of kings and bishops) and at Boxgrove Priory, close by.

Eight of the Amberley Panels survive and there are excellent copies of three of them in the castle. The precise date at which the bishop commissioned them is unknown, but we have a tantalising clue. In the many other examples of interior decoration carried out for the bishop by Bernard we find the monograms of Henry VIII and his first wife, Catherine of Aragon, whereas on the Amberley Panels only Sherborne's initials appear. Henry visited Sherborne at Chichester – and perhaps was invited to Amberley too – in 1526. This was soon after Henry's decision to divorce Catherine, and the purpose of the visit may well have been to sound out the bishop on this thorny issue. Did Sherborne have the Queens' Room painted for the occasion?

He certainly needed to be cautious, because the religious upheavals

A large painting by Lambert Bernard in Chichester Cathedral shows Henry VIII confirming to Bishop Sherborne the royal protection of Chichester – a piece of propaganda which reveals the bishop's shrewdness in his dealings with the monarch in dangerous times.

HENRY VIII
A GREAT ALL-ROUNDER

Most portraits of Henry VIII show him to be a massively overweight figure, but in his youth he was an impressive athlete who also excelled in scholarly and artistic pursuits – he played the lute and the harpsichord, and is credited with writing and setting to music the haunting English love song 'Greensleeves'. Henry wrote a book attacking Martin Luther's reformist ideas, and the Pope rewarded him with the title 'Defender of the Faith', which is still borne by English sovereigns. Soon afterwards, however, the refusal of the Pope to grant Henry a divorce led to the rift with Rome which created an independent Church of England and led to the dissolution of the monasteries. Henry's ruthless streak (he had six wives, two of whom he had executed) eventually made him unpopular, but he had followed his father in modernising the state and strengthening the power of the crown, and his daughter Elizabeth would become perhaps the greatest English monarch of all.

which would split the English church from Rome and suppress the monasteries were already well advanced. Henry was determined on the divorce, and anyone who stood in his way was doomed. The powerful Cardinal Wolsey was charged with high treason, dying in disgrace before the scaffold could claim his life – and Bishop Sherborne, an opponent of the Reformation, was one of Wolsey's supporters.

Not surprisingly, Sherborne believed in playing his cards close to his chest. Now an old man, he could surely be forgiven for replying to the question of the royal divorce with a careful silence. A large Bernard painting in the cathedral's south transept, depicting Henry VIII confirming to the bishop the royal protection of Chichester, has been described as 'an engaging diplomatic myth'. It displays both Sherborne's shrewdness and Henry's willingness to grant favours to achieve his ends.

Henry had himself proclaimed Supreme Head of the Church of England in 1531, and the events which followed were soon to sever Amberley's close ties with its ecclesiastical owners: indeed, Robert Sherborne, whose favourite rooms still exist in the castle's (private) east wing, was the last bishop of Chichester to enjoy the pleasures of the Amberley retreat.

Between 1536 and 1540 all of the monastic religious houses in England were closed, the reformers regarding them as backward-looking, covetous and corrupt. Their gold and silver plate, jewellery and other valuable items were looted for the royal treasury, and their buildings were razed to the ground. In Sussex the great Cluniac priory at Lewes, one of the greatest monasteries in England with a church larger than Chichester Cathedral, was demolished on the instructions of Henry's first minister, Thomas Cromwell. The abbeys at Battle, Bayham and Robertsbridge (all in the east of the county) suffered a similar fate. Only those buildings which could claim to perform a vital local service survived: the monk's church at Boxgrove, for example, had also served as the parish church, while the Greyfriars' chancel at Chichester (in what is now Priory Park) became the shire hall. Within a generation three quarters of the land and possession of the religious houses was in the hands of the nobility and the rising middle class of gentry, merchants and lawyers.

The reformed Church itself, by contrast, was safe 'under new ownership', but it was much changed, nonetheless, by the new intellectual climate. The bishops found that they had less time for leisure, dividing their time between their local ecclesiastical business and national politics in London. Riding ostentatiously to hounds would hardly have suited the temper of the times. Amberley, like their other retreats, became nothing more than a source of income to the bishops of Chichester, and the cathedral chapter now confirmed leases to a succession of tenants and sub-tenants.

The first lease on record – in 1538, for a period of 21 years – was to William Shelley and William Goring, with William Earnley being the sub-tenant. Earnley was obviously an up-and-coming man, since he had already leased the bishop's palace at Cakeham. He was giving vigorous support to that architect of religious change, Thomas Cromwell, and he and Goring were among those responsible for what Sherborne, had he still been alive, would have regarded as an act of brute sacrilege – the destruction of the fabulous shrine of St Richard in the cathedral in protest against the Popish belief in the prayers of saints. In 1577 his family were evidently still sub-tenants, because we discover that Edward, the son of Richard and Elizabeth Earnley of Cakeham, was baptised in the castle chapel – the last time that the chapel is mentioned in cathedral documents.

By this time the country had been ruled by three further monarchs. Protestantism had flourished in the brief reign of the 'boy king', Edward VI (1547–53), but 'Bloody' Queen Mary required even less time (1553–1558) to turn the reforms on their head – instigating a period of Catholic terror in which hundreds of Protestants were martyred for their beliefs. More than two dozen victims were burned to death in Sussex, 17 of them at Lewes. A poem of the time, published surreptitiously, ends:

> *When one fire at Lewes brought them to death*
> *We wished for our Elizabeth.*

That wish was granted, for Mary's sister Elizabeth came to the throne in 1558 and ruled for 45 years, a period which constituted a prosperous, golden age – an age, among much else, of English sea power abroad and of the literature of Shakespeare and his contemporaries at home.

It was also, however, a time of continual tensions and dangers, with the queen's life under threat from the conspiracies of Catholic-inspired assassins. In 1572, the Duke of Norfolk – the most powerful nobleman in the land – was executed for plotting, with the blessing of the Pope,

'GLORIANA'

The daughter of Henry VIII and Ann Boleyn, Elizabeth was a highly educated woman (she spoke five languages besides English) who was also known for her musical ability, her graceful dancing and her skill at archery. Her admiring courtiers referred to her as 'Gloriana', while to the man and woman in the street she was Good Queen Bess. A tough and adroit politician in dangerous times, she also knew how to turn a speech.

'Though I be a woman, I have as good a courage answerable to my place as ever my father had,' she told a deputation of both Houses of Parliament. 'I am your anointed Queen. I will never be by violence constrained to do anything. I thank God I am endued with such qualities that if I were turned out of the realm in my petticoat, I were able to live in any place in Christendom.'

The former Bishop of Chichester, Eric Kemp, unveiling the Amberley Panel reproductions at Amberley Castle.

to marry the Catholic Mary Queen of Scots. In 1587, Mary herself lost her head. And then, in 1588, the great Spanish Armada set sail to put Protestant England to the ultimate test. It was in this very year that Elizabeth took a 50-year lease on Amberley Castle.

For the people of Amberley and the villages nearby the summer of 1588 was one of apprehension. Not only was the Spanish fleet on its way, but the county was horribly unprepared. A survey the previous year had found that long stretches of the coastline were unprotected, while established fortifications were in a bad state of repair. On the night of Friday July 19, beacons were fired on Sussex hilltops to warn that the Armada was on its way, the news being carried eastwards along the coast and, via Ditchling and Crowborough, inland to London. On July 25 the cry went up at Selsey as the first ships were sighted. Lookouts on the tower of Chichester Cathedral ordered the ringing of the bells.

At Amberley, vulnerably upriver from the coast, the news must have arrived fitfully. The huge Armada had advanced in a crescent formation, stretching all of seven miles across the channel. Harried by the English navy, it had later become becalmed off Fairlight, at the eastern end of Sussex, before sailing away towards Calais. And then – alas, St Michael's had no bells to ring in those days! – came news that the Spanish had been defeated, with the survivors limping home.

Elizabeth, who had good friends at nearby Parham, leased the castle to a series of sub-tenants. Although we know the names of some of the principal lessees in the following years, we are largely dependent upon the parish registers for clues as to who was living in the castle and its place in the social network of the county. In the light of the troubles which were to follow, the names have an ominously Royalist ring.

In 1606, for instance, a daughter of Walter Dobell of Street Place, near Ditchling, was buried at Amberley. Dobell bought various properties from the Gorings in the early 17th century, and we know that in the 1630s the Amberley lease was held jointly by a Henry Goring and a Henry Barttelot. Richard Lewkenor, who was buried at Arundel in 1626, was described as 'of Amberley', and two of his grandchildren were baptised at Amberley church in 1617 and 1620. The Lewkenors must have succeeded the Earnleys as 'live-in' tenants. A Thomas Lewkenor would later be described as 'menial servant' to Sir Edward Ford of Uppark, the Royalist commander who took control of Chichester early in the war.

In 1639 John Billingshurst, perhaps a steward or caretaker of the Lewkenors, was buried at Amberley, and a surviving inventory of his belongings shows that he was living in a suite of ten rooms here. Under the heading 'The Queens' Chamber' were three good beds and other furniture: Bishop Sherborne's 'painted ladies' were still there, but the grand reception chamber was now nothing more than a bedroom. There were another three beds, but of much less value, in the 'haukesmew' – presumably a room where falcons had been kept in cages at a time when Amberley had been clangorous with the noise and bustle of a hunting lodge. Such pleasures, however, were now in the past. The clouds of war were gathering, and on this occasion even Amberley Castle would not be spared.

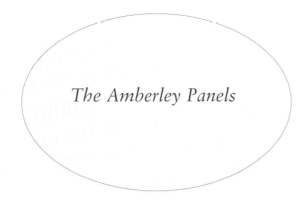

The Amberley Panels

In choosing to depict exemplary pagan women on his walls at Amberley Castle, Bishop Sherborne was in tune with Renaissance thinking. For one thing higher class women were now encouraged to excel in intellectual and artistic pursuits (which were, at the same time, a reflection on the taste of wisdom of their husbands), while it was also being argued by the new breed of neo-classisists that the best men and women of former times had much to teach contemporary Christian society about the virtuous life. Dante located them in limbo rather than in the utter darkness of hell.

A view of what was already called the Queens' Room in around 1840 suggests that the panels originally formed a gallery looking down into the chamber. A travel guide of 1819 actually recorded 'ten kings and their queens, and portraits of six warriors', while another report of that time spoke of warriors carved on the ceiling.

Bernard's panels seem to have been removed some time in the 19th century, because in 1848 the then owner of West Dean House found them hanging in his home and returned them to Amberley. More recently they were acquired by Chichester District Council, with help from the National Heritage Memorial Fund, and they are now on display at the Pallant House gallery in the city.

'As a time capsule of English provincial, domestic, political and propagandic art,' the art historian Karen Coke has written, 'the works of Lambert Bernard, and the Amberley Panels in particular, are the only remaining body of early 16th century work left to us in England. They are of tremendous art historical importance, both on a provincial and national scale, and should be considered an irreplaceable contribution to our region and country's heritage.'

RIGHT Queen Thamoris (or Thomyris) was queen of the Massagetae or Scit, a strong, cruel and barbaric tribe from a cold and arid region (the 'hydeous pepell of Cytees'). The great King Cyrus invaded her lands and tricked her son into a demeaning defeat. Thamoris avenged her son's death by subduing Cyrus in a subsequent battle, beheading his nobles in front of him before executing Cyrus himself.

Cassandra noct data paticina

OPPOSITE PAGE Queen Zenobia (probably: her inscription has not survived). As queen of the Palmyrenes she was the most virtuous of all pagan women: chaste, learned and well versed in the arts of war. She extended her realm through Asia Minor, most of Syria and Egypt. In this painting she is identified by her helmet, which she invariably wore when addressing her troops. 'Wondre fayre and swete for to behold', she was famed for the blackness of her eyes and the whiteness of her teeth.

ABOVE The Trojan princess Cassandra, daughter of Priam and Hecuba and sister of Hector. Her gift of prophecy was doomed never to be believed (although it was invariably correct) because she spurned the amorous advances of Apollo.

Civil War

It is the winter of 1644 and Oliver Cromwell's Parliamentary troops are at the gates of the castle, about to dismantle the battlements and lay waste the Great Hall. Perhaps if John Goring had kept his head down like the rest of his family the slighting of the medieval walls might have been prevented, but this would have been against his nature. Goring is a firebrand Royalist.

Two years ago, fired up with the news of his cousin George declaring for Charles I in Portsmouth, he had loudly promised commissions to all and sundry if they would join the cause. And when he had heard of another cousin among the Royalists who had taken Arundel, he supplied firearms to one of their captains and tried to recruit Amberley people, crying 'Join me, and no Roundhead rogues will ever have my castle!'

Now he is about to get his comeuppance – and so, sadly, is the building itself.

With the eastern two-thirds of Sussex broadly sympathetic to the Parliamentarian cause, it was the predominantly Royalist western part of the county close to Amberley which saw most of the action during the Civil War which broke out in 1642. Cromwell was anxious to control Sussex, because it offered a potential escape route for the king and, more pressing still, because it was vital that arms produced by the iron industry of the Weald should not fall into Royalist hands.

The key towns were Chichester and Arundel. In Chichester there was a marked conflict of allegiances: the merchant classes rallied to Cromwell, while resident clergy and the local gentry were Royalist in their sympathies. Supporters of the two sides actually trained in close proximity during the autumn of 1642 until, in mid-November, Sir Edward Ford of Uppark took control. Ford then marched towards Lewes, but was defeated at Haywards Heath.

ABOVE Sir William Waller.

OPPOSITE PAGE The handsome staircase with its carved and turned balusters was installed at Amberley Castle by James Butler once the smoke of the English Civil War had cleared.

Reproductions of two of the Amberley Panels can be seen hanging on the staircase wall.

A NATION DIVIDED

The first skirmish of the Civil War in Sussex was at Haywards Heath in December 1642, when a Royalist (Cavalier) army under Sir Edward Ford was routed by a smaller Parliamentary (Roundhead) force.

At root lay a confrontation between the stubborn Catholic Charles I and a Protestant parliament increasingly flexing its muscles. Mercifully the fighting was limited to isolated areas of the country, and the bloodshed was relatively light.

The decisive national battles were in 1644, when victory at Marston Moor gave Parliament all the north of England, and 1645, when Cromwell's 'New Model' Army crushed the king's forces at Naseby. The capitulation of Oxford in 1646 effectively brought the war to a close. An uprising in 1648, when the Scots mounted a doomed attempt to rescue the king, only served to seal his fate.

Charles I was beheaded on January 30, 1649.

Sir William Waller, Cromwell's favourite lieutenant, was the man charged with subduing the west of Sussex. He first took Arundel Castle, which was garrisoned by a hundred Royalist troops, and then beseiged Chichester. It surrendered, after just eight days, in December 1642 – and the Roundheads moved in.

The Dean of Chichester (hardly a neutral observer), wrote of Waller's troops: 'Their first business was to plunder the cathedral church. They left not so much as a cushion for the pulpit or a chalice for the blessed sacrament.' As they broke the organ with pole-axes, he wrote, 'they scoffed "harke how the organs goe".'

The soldiers broke the table of the Ten Commandments 'into small shivers', scattering the leaves of prayer books around. They defaced Lambert Bernard's pictures of bishops and kings and 'ran down the church with the swords drawn, defacing the monuments of the dead, hacking and hewing the seats and stalls, scratching and scraping the painted walls, Sir William Waller and the rest of the commanders standing by as spectators and approvers of these impious barbarities.'

Although 1643 was relatively quiet, the leader of the Parliamentarian gentry, Colonel Herbert Morley of Glynde, wrote prophetically to the Speaker of the House of Commons: 'This approaching clowd I feare may raise a storme in Sussex, which county is full of newters and malignants, and I have ever observed newters to turn malignants upon such occasions.'

In the December of that year the Royalists under Lord Hopton swept in from Hampshire, seized the lightly-garrisoned houses of Stansted and Cowdray and forced Arundel to surrender. Hopton installed a garrison of a thousand men at Arundel, prompting a swift and decisive response. Waller now raised all of ten thousand troops and laid seige to the castle, draining Swanbourne Lake (which features in the Domesday Book) in order to deny water to its garrison. He placed cannon on the roof of the parish church, and inflicted such heavy damage on the castle that parts of it would lie in ruins for years. The victory earned Waller the title of major-general, a title he held over Sussex, Hampshire, Surrey and Kent.

The Royalist forces included Sir Edward Bishop of Parham, his wife, his 17-year-old daughter and her husband. After three weeks, with negotiations underway for lifting the seige, Waller invited Lady Bishop, her daughters and other female relatives to dine with him – a touch of chivalry amid the noise of war.

The people of Amberley must have been uncomfortably aware of the vulnerability of their own castle, and terrified of what unruly soldiers might do in their unprotected village. Although Sussex escaped the heavy bloodshed of a Marston Moor, the war threatened to ruin farmers who were obliged to provide food for troops camped on their land, while tenants and labourers found themselves pressed into armed service. A petition of the time tells of 'the country far and wide ransacked for bread, rents unpaid; two sets of hungry soldiery in turn masters; church, cottage mansion and park alike pillaged; the squires in gaol, the parsons and farmers fined . . .'.

John Goring, living in Amberley Castle with his widowed mother, was the son of a second marriage, his father's estate having been inherited by an older son. Was his wild streak perhaps exaggerated by a nothing-to-lose mentality? In November 1644, with the war now over, there was a move by Parliamentary supporters to pull down houses which had harboured opponents of their cause. In the event most of these buildings were either garrisoned or simply left empty, with their outer walls and doors removed – but we can imagine the relish with which Cromwell's soldiers made an example of Amberley and

The rueful Cavalier. John Goring was powerless to prevent the destruction of Amberley Castle by Roundhead troops.

WILD JOHN GORING

John Goring had undeniable spirit. In 1648, with Charles I only months from the scaffold, he put his name to a petition for disbanding the army and reducing taxes. It had already taken a band of soldiers from Arundel to get any money out of him at all.

Even after Charles I had been executed, Goring (now living at Greatham) was denounced for falling on his knees in a local inn and drinking a toast to Prince Charles and the downfall of Parliament – made up, he said, of 'rogues, knaves and upstart gentlemen'.

'A very troublesome fellow in the county,' was the verdict of Major General Goffe, 'but I thinke able to doe little hurt, he is such a kind of madd heady fellow.'

Goring. No record survives of the destruction, but we can be sure that the men he had called 'roundhead rogues' flattened the Great Hall, destroyed most of the crenellations, set the roofs ablaze and rendered parts of the castle virtually uninhabitable.

The final indignity, again unsurprising, was John Goring's official eviction. In 1648 the parliamentary sequestrators sold the castle to James Butler, a London cloth merchant with an eye to the main chance and a comfortable retirement. He paid £3,341 14s 4d – about £230,000 at today's prices.

If Butler felt secure in his new possession, events would prove otherwise. A brief second civil war in 1648 had ended with the defeat of the king's supporters and the execution of Charles I – unbending and dignified to the last. (Seven Sussex men were among the 49 who signed his death warrant.) Parliament was supreme, with Cromwell established as Lord Protector.

The Scots, however, were determined to restore a Stuart to the throne in the person of the dead king's son, the future Charles II. After Cromwell defeated their army at the Battle of Worcester in 1651, Charles fled south with a reward of a thousand pounds on his head. His one hope of survival was to pass undetected through a countryside bristling with Roundhead soldiers and find a ship's captain who would carry him to safety in France. Colonel George Gounter of Racton, north-west of Chichester, played a leading role in the heart-stopping drama of what became known as the Great Escape, and he later wrote of accompanying Charles and the Royalist Lord Wilmot from Hampshire, through the west of Sussex and on to Brighton.

Riding over the downs above Stansted Park, the royal party turned their horses east through Kingley Vale. From Stoke Down they had a fine view of Chichester, and Charles – who had had his hair shorn as a disguise, and was answering to the name of Will Jackson – deplored the damage that had been caused by the Roundhead army nine years earlier. Above Goodwood they stopped to admire the Tudor mansion Halnaker House (today a ruin) down to their left.

Eventually they approached Arundel, where they narrowly avoided coming face-to-face with the garrison commander, who was out exercising his horse. Alarmed, they turned north to the river crossing at Houghton, where they took a snack of 'neat's tongues' and a stoup of ale. The route passed so close to Amberley that some of the locals

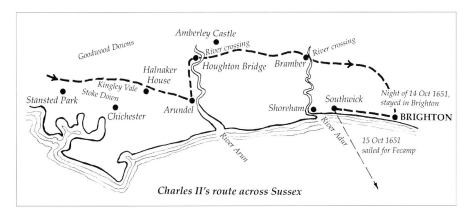

Charles II's route across Sussex

Charles II.

almost certainly saw Charles and mistook him for Gounter's servant. Did the future king lament the dismantled walls of Amberley Castle as he rode by? Did he reflect on his father's arrogance and folly, and determine to rule more wisely himself should that day ever arrive?

In *Highways and Byways in Sussex*, E.V. Lucas writes: 'And so to Amberley, where in Sir John Briscoe's castle the King slept.' Briscoe (see page 63) acquired the lease only in 1683, and a footnote admits that the evidence for the future monarch's stay at Amberley is lacking, but it is at least a tantalising might-have-been.

Charles and his companions suffered another scare at Bramber, at the crossing of the River Adur. 'Being come to Bramber,' Gounter wrote later, 'we found the streets full of soldiers both sides of the houses.' They considered turning back, but thought this would look suspicious, so they crossed the bridge – and immediately heard a cacophonous clattering of hooves as dozens of soldiers swept by, almost tumbling them from their saddles.

They finally reached the coast, where Nicholas Tettersell was ready with his coal brig *The Surprise*. Within nine years Charles II was on the throne, and all the estates taken from the church, including Amberley Castle, were immediately returned. The Bishop of Chichester, Henry King – a former chaplain to both James I and Charles I – had his estates returned to him, while many Puritan clergymen who had been forced upon local parishes after the Civil War either resigned or were ejected.

There is no record as to whether James Butler got his money back, but he took out a long lease with the bishop the following year. He and his Flemish wife had been spending time at the castle, and two of their

The outer defences of Amberley Castle were dismantled at the end of the Civil War, and ruined walls can still be seen in the grounds today.

daughters were christened in the parish church. Despite the damage inflicted by Waller's soldiers, enough must have remained relatively untouched to convert into a comfortable family home, because Butler had taken his place in Sussex society and become a magistrate. The fine staircase with its carved and turned balusters dates from this period.

The second James Butler, who took over the lease from his father, embroiled the Bishop of Chichester in a series of expensive law suits in chancery, attempting to get better terms for a new lease. Bishop Carleton accused him and his father of having reduced the value of Houghton Chasse from £2,000 to just £400, of trying to 'trample' on him with unreasonable proposals and of using his 'great estate and great puff' to force his terms on the church.

The arguments dragged on, made worse by the fact that Butler was siding with the dean and canons at the cathedral, who were also in conflict with the bishop. Carleton, who accused Butler of 'severely rude, scornfull and insolent behaviour', was clearly not to be brow-beaten.

'He has the wrong sow by the ear,' he wrote to the Archbishop of Canterbury.

In 1683 the lease was bought by Sir John Briscoe. The hunting scene in the Queens' Room, flanked by the arms of Charles II and his queen, Catherine of Braganza, dates from his time but we know very little about Sir John, except that he came from Northampton, served as a magistrate and was buried in the parish church in 1723. Perhaps the commissioning of the painting was an attempt to distance himself from the rebellious spirit of his predecessors, extravagantly showing his loyalty to the restored monarchy by 'nailing his colours to the mast'.

THE WILLIAM PENN CONNECTION

The Butlers passed on their religious vehemence from father to son. In 1707, after they had left Amberley, the third James Butler bought Warminghurst Place, some 5 miles north-east of Amberley, from William Penn. He demolished the old house, vowing 'to leave no trace of the old Quaker'.

Penn had been given a royal charter for the land of Pennsylvania in 1681, and it was at Warminghurst that he drafted a constitution for the new state that was a forerunner of the US Constitution. He sailed for America in 1682 with other Sussex emigrants, returning two years later to help his fellow Quakers fight persecution. He helped found a meeting house (now known as the Blue Idol) in a farmhouse at Coolham, eight miles from Amberley. His daughter was married, and later buried, there.

The hunting scene in the Queens' Room dates from the tenancy (1683–1723) of Sir John Briscoe, and is flanked by the arms of Charles II and Queen Catherine of Braganza.

West Court of Amberly Castle

As the world beyond was transformed beyond measure – as Britain forged an empire and launched an industrial revolution; as, step by step, the levers of power shifted from the crown to the people through parliament – life at Amberley Castle seems, in retrospect, unchanging. Throughout the eighteenth and nineteenth centuries the building became little more than a glorified farmhouse (perhaps feeling rather *too* glorified for the tenant who, in 1779, had to pay window tax on all of 34 windows), and illustrations of the castle are generally of more interest than its occupiers during this period.

In 1737, for instance, an engraving of the building by Samuel and Nathaniel Buck was published. This highly romanticised view shows little evidence of damage or decay – surely the Bucks must have imaginatively rebuilt those crenellations! – although there are hints of neglect in the greenery which protrudes above the walls to the south and the missing tracery from a window to the south of the gateway.

In 1788 Samuel Grimm, employed by the antiquarian Sir William Burrell to sketch the churches and principal houses of Sussex for a proposed history, arrived at Amberley with his easel and box of pencils. The Peacheys of Fittleworth, eventually Lords Selsey, had by then begun what was to be long tenancy. Grimm made four tinted drawings of the castle, including two views inside the walls which seem closer to reality than the Buck engraving.

Samuel Grimm drew four pictures of the castle altogether, including ABOVE the view from the south, with the main gateway on the right, and, on the OPPOSITE PAGE, a view looking north-west towards the ruins of the Great Hall and the pantry and buttery entrances.

Seven years later several drawings were published in *The Gentleman's Magazine*. Although these are too small to include much detail, the accompanying description of the castle is interesting:

'It is built on a rock, is of a parallelogram form, with an entrance on the south under a gateway between two small round towers, with grooves for a portcullis. It is defended on the south by a foss over which is a bridge leading to the principal entrance; and on the north and west sides by the low rocky precipice it stands on. It does not appear ever to have been of great strength, but the ruins of an arch within the walls show the architecture to have been light and elegant . . . Its present owner, under the bishop, with the appendage of a large farm, is Lord Silsea, and the castle is degraded to a farmhouse . . . the clump of trees

Inner court of Kenilworth Castle

An engraving of 1820 by J. Grieg
from a drawing by T. Higham.

A photograph of the ivy-clad
gateway in the late 19th century,
with the tenant farmer in the
foreground.

In 1846 the Sussex Archaeological Society paid an official visit to Amberley Castle, and this record of the event appeared in the *Illustrated London News*.

seen on the top of the hill in the background is called Fittleworth Tilt, and serves as a sea-mark.'

The census records, every ten years from 1841 to 1891, suggest that the castle buildings were often occupied by more than one household, including the Harwood family for over fifty years. From walking about the village it is clear that the crumbling walls were used as an unofficial quarry, and one has a vivid mental image of needy local people sallying forth at dusk with barrows and carts to collect stone to build or repair their cottages.

Amberley Castle was now at its lowest ebb since Roundhead soldiers had dismantled its defences, but salvation was at hand – and from the grandest of all possible neighbours.

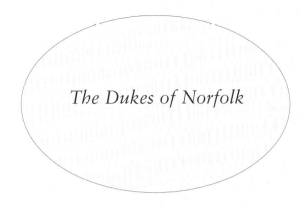

The Dukes of Norfolk

Sir John Howard was created the first Duke of Norfolk and Earl Marshal of England in 1483 (both the dukedom – now the senior in our peerage – and the great office of state have descended with few interruptions to the present day), but the Arundel connection dates from 1555. In that year Thomas Howard, the 4th duke, married the heiress of the Fitzalan family who had been earls of Arundel for nearly three hundred years.

Although closely related to Elizabeth I, Howard was nevertheless under great suspicion at a time of political and religious turmoil because of his Roman Catholic beliefs, and in 1572 he was beheaded on Tower Hill in London for plotting to marry Mary Queen of Scots. A rosary which she gave him is one of the treasures of Arundel Castle.

His son Philip, the 13th Earl of Arundel, had inherited the castle from his Fitzalan grandfather. He entertained Elizabeth there in 1584, but he was a zealous Catholic and spent the last ten years of his life in the Tower, expecting execution at any moment. After his death in

1595 (he had eaten a dish of poisoned teal), he was beatified as the Blessed Philip and finally canonised in 1970. He has a shrine in the Cathedral of Our Lady and St Philip Howard at Arundel.

Philip Howard's son, the 14th earl, was deprived of most of his estates during Elizabeth's reign. Although James I restored the earldom of Arundel to him, he not surprisingly kept a low profile politically and spent much of his life abroad: the famous Arundel Marbles, which he collected in Italy, can be seen in the background of his portrait in the castle's drawing room. It was his grandson, the 16th Earl of Arundel who became the 5th Duke of Norfolk after the restoration of Charles II in 1660, while a younger brother became a cardinal.

Because Catholics were long barred from sitting in Parliament and holding public office, the activities of the Howard family were until Victorian times largely restricted to managing their estates, but the 12th Duke (1815-1842) was allowed to perform his hereditary duties as earl marshal in

spite of being a Roman Catholic, eventually being allowed to take up his seat in the House of Lords.

As earls marshal, the Howards have been ex-officio heads of the College of Arms, the highest authority on royal ceremonial, and as such in charge of coronations and other great state events. Bernard, the popular 16th Duke (1917-1975), organised the state funerals of George V and George VI, the coronations of George VI and Elizabeth II and the funeral of Sir Winston Churchill. After his death, his equally popular widow, Duchess Lavinia, succeeded him as Lord Lieutenant of West Sussex – the first woman to be appointed to such a high office.

RIGHT The bronze monument to Henry, the 15th Duke of Norfolk, lies among the tombs of other Earls of Norfolk in the Fitzalan Chapel at Arundel Castle. Formerly the chancel of the parish church, it was sold to the Fitzalan family at the dissolution of the monasteries. This Roman Catholic place of worship can be seen through a glass screen at the eastern end of the (Anglican) parish church, and can be entered by visitors to the castle.

Arundel Castle, home of the Dukes of Norfolk, lies five miles south of Amberley Castle. This places both castles on the River Arun, strategically at the north and south gaps in the South Downs.

Enter the Duke

As Henry, 15th Duke of Norfolk, signs the document which gives him the freehold of Amberley Castle is he aware of a delicious irony? Here he is, in 1893, the descendant of the man once excommunicated by the bishop for hunting in his chase, bringing to an end the many centuries of ecclesiastical ownership.

It is a double irony, however, for the bishop's fine castle has fallen upon hard times – and Henry will be the man to turn the decades-long tide of neglect and decay.

The duke had inherited his title while still a schoolboy. His father, once described as an 'aristocratic version of the Salvation Army', had devoted much of his time and income to good works. Deeply interested in architecture, he had just employed an architect to begin the ambitious project of restoring Arundel Castle when, in 1860 at the age of just 45, he died of a liver disease.

Young Henry, barred from attending an English university because he was a Catholic, received his education abroad – some of it on a 'grand tour'. Like his father, he developed a love of architecture, amassing a wonderful collection of books on the subject and becoming an acknowledged expert on the Gothic style.

Like his father, too, he determined to rebuild Arundel Castle, employing C.A. Buckler as his architect and almost bankrupting himself in the process. The duke knew his tragedies (his young wife died in 1887, and their blind and epileptic son, Philip, in 1902) but he found late happiness in a second marriage in 1904. It was some four years after this that he turned his attention to his other castle at Amberley.

The duke restored the gatehouse and some of the crenellations on the west wall. No detailed account of his work at the castle has been found, although in 1909 more than £2,000 was spent on it, with another £700

Henry, 15th Duke of Norfolk

OPPOSITE PAGE The 15th Duke repaired the battlements by the entrance to Amberley Castle. Note the 'tidemark' of new stone.

ABOVE The Amberley Castle gatehouse before the Duke of Norfolk's restoration of the battlements.

BBOVE RIGHT The north and west walls from the Wild Brooks in about 1900.

paid to Messrs Burrell and Standen in 1913. Not everyone was happy:

'I think you cannot be aware how much the ruins of the castle are being interfered with,' a woman from Kent who was staying in Amberley wrote to the duke's land agent. 'Wooden doors are being inserted by masons in the beautiful pointed archways and the old stone cut and hacked away to fit them – by whose orders I know not. Surely no private person can have the right to alter and deface historic ruins such as these.'

The agent was rather curt in his response: 'The restorations at Amberley Castle are being carried out under the Duke of Norfolk's personal supervision, and although I am constantly over I have not as yet seen anything out of character with the original design and certainly nothing to deface the ruins.'

It is possible that, for all the duke's best intentions, his enthusiasm for Gothic architecture followed common Victorian practice in destroying some of the evidence for earlier forms. The fact remains that he was responsible for a welcome refurbishment of the castle that later owners were keen to emulate.

LEFT Thomas and Evelyn Emmet at the christening of their daughter Lavinia in August 1924. They bought Amberley Castle a year later, and their four children were brought up here.

BELOW The Emmet family playing tennis at Amberley.

In 1925 the castle was sold to Thomas and Evelyn Emmet, who were eager to effect some 're-conditioning'. The price paid was £10,000. A few years earlier Walter Peckham had carried out some excavations at the castle with the help of another noted antiquarian, L.F. Salzman, and the Emmets now invited him back for a second look. Peckham examined the stonework more closely and revised some of his earlier conclusions, although he never managed to complete a fresh report.

The work carried out by the Emmets involved a number of areas – the wash house, east wing, court room wing and cellars – and Peckham was able to examine foundations and areas that had not been opened up before. From this, he revised his original opinion that the buildings dated from roughly three periods, now managing to identify at least five.

Evelyn Emmet was particularly fond of the garden, which she created once the rebuilding work had been completed. This included a tennis court and (a homage, no doubt, to memories of the Emmets time in Italy) the planting of the tall cypress trees which are today, alas, almost at the end of their lives. Box and topiary were especial favourites of the

The antiquarian Walter Peckham drew this ground plan of the castle in 1921, but revised his findings after being invited to Amberley once again by the Emmets.

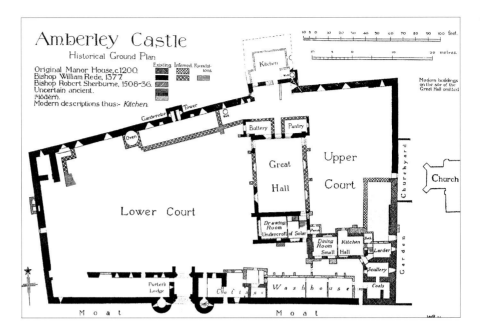

family, too. The Emmets opened the gardens only rarely (usually for charity), and in later years, when the family had grown up and left, Evelyn could often be seen tending the gardens on her own, dressed in combat fatigues.

We are now within living memory, and Ann Money-Coutts, the youngest of the Emmets' four children, recalls it as 'the most wonderful place to grow up in. It was very enclosing, but we spent our lives climbing the walls, chasing each other round them and playing games of historical make-believe. One never felt frightened at Amberley, because the place had a lovely, friendly atmosphere.'

Mrs Emmet measured her children and grandchildren, and recorded their heights on the doorframe of the nursery – now the entrance to the Rye and Chichester rooms.

As for the building work: 'Oh, all the time! The back of the house was in a mess, and the present dining room and Queens' Room were created just before the war out of what had been the chapel.'

Ann's father, Thomas, died of tuberculosis in 1934 when she was less than two years old, and her mother, the remarkable Evelyn, now combined a busy life at Amberley with a steadily advancing political career as, successively, a West Sussex county councillor, a member of London County Council, a British delegate to the United Nations and

**THE GREAT FOOTPATH
DISPUTE**

For generations local people had been accustomed to take a short cut from Amberley churchyard through the castle grounds to the Arundel-Storrington road, and when Thomas Emmet decided to close it there was a predictable outcry.

Amberley Parish Council and Thakeham Rural District Council claimed that the route was a public right of way, but in October 1927 an independent arbitrator decided in favour of the Emmets.

The photograph shows the footpath running in front of the house. The large doorway in what is now the library was at that time the main entrance.

ABOVE LEFT The Emmets carried out extensive improvements to the castle. This photograph shows scaffolding erected in December 1927.

LEFT It's July 1928, and the work has been completed – including an extension behind the Library, now known as the Adam Room, which takes its name from the splendid fireplace.

The Court Room when the
Emmets owned the castle.

A festive occasion on the lawn,
1927. The Emmets brought back
family life to Amberley Castle.
    Thomas Emmet is second on
the left, his wife Evelyn fourth on
the left.

Lavinia Emmet wearing a bridesmaid's dress in 1927, before the facade of the building was altered.

The photograph on the left is of a similar view, although the path, relaid in 2000, now looks as it did when Lavinia was a child.

Evelyn Emmet organised pageants to celebrate the jubilee of George V and the coronation of George VI, involving all the village children. The original script was adapted for the coronation of our present queen in 1953:

Dear friends and neighbours, who have come today
To join us in our village celebration,
We hope you will enjoy our pageant play
In honour of our good Queen's Coronation . . .

then Conservative member of parliament for East Grinstead before entering the House of Lords as Baroness Emmet of Amberley.

During the Second World War the castle was used as a depot for supplies to those bombed out of towns in the region – particularly Portsmouth and Southampton. The main rooms were piled high with clothes, dried milk, cocoa, first aid boxes and blankets, while such was Lady Emmet's energy that, as well as running the Women's Voluntary Service in West Sussex, she also managed the large farm at Amberley Castle.

In July, 1945, Princess Elizabeth (now Queen Elizabeth II) visited the castle for the 21st birthday of the eldest Emmet daughter, Lavinia, while staying with the Duke and Duchess of Norfolk at Arundel Castle. (Her grandparents, George V and Queen Mary, had spent the day there in 1929 while staying at Bognor Regis, where the king was recovering from a serious illness). It was fitting, therefore, that the Amberley Pageant was repeated, with suitable amendments, for Elizabeth II's coronation in 1953.

In that year the 17-year-old Ivy West (now Reed) came down to Amberley with her parents, living at the Old Post Office, near the church. Her father Alfred was gardener at the castle, and Ivy worked in the house during the morning.

'It was a lovely, peaceful place. I remember going through the churchyard to the castle in the morning. My mother couldn't work because she had Parkinson's disease. Mrs Emmet could be abrupt, but she was fair – you knew where you stood – and she would visit my mother and sit with her.'

In 1962 Alfred West collapsed and died in the grounds he tended.

The Emmets' son Christopher, who took over the estate farm in 1949, had forged a family tie with the neighbouring Duke of Norfolk. His wife Miranda (now Lady Miranda Emmet) was a cousin of the then duke, Bernard, and is the present duke's sister.

'We kept a herd of pedigree Jerseys, and we had a fleet of electric vans selling milk in the surrounding villages. It never made a great profit, but it paid its way. I liked being 'hands-on', and I had my horses to ride, too. I got to know a lot of the villagers, pushing my children in the push-chair to the ice-cream shop and so on. They were lovely people, and I still visit several of them today.'

Lady Miranda, widowed in 1996, also remembers the building work.

'My mother-in-law was always planning something! She loved her garden, and she was a great builder. I remember her clearing the moat so that it looked more like the real thing, and she installed a tennis court in the garden. She never stopped still.'

After Lady Emmet's death in 1980, the farms and houses scattered round the estate were sold off separately, while the castle itself (together with its outbuildings and some 11 acres of fenced fields to the south) was purchased by Hollis MacLure Baker from Michigan. He had inherited a well-known reproduction furniture company founded by his grandfather, and in his retirement he made a hobby of restoring castles. Amberley was his fifth.

He later wrote a book, *Five Castles Are Enough*, in which he relates

What the doctor ordered: a bottle of champagne with the Amberley Castle logo on it sits between two bottles of the milk produced at the castle farm.

his Amberley experience, often with a quiet humour: 'the arrangement of the rooms and passages in [the east] wing was so circuitous that it took a year or two before we could get through without getting lost.'

The Bakers shut up the east wing, using the manor house as their living quarters. A great many repairs and improvements to the comfort of the place were made during this period, while a major operation was undertaken to improve the castle's security. Having already built a portcullis in a French chateau, Mr Baker – with the assistance of craftsman Mike Smith from Pulborough – now set about doing the same for Amberley Castle.

'We realised that an electrically operated portcullis would be much easier for us. It would have been very difficult, day in and day out, to get out of the car and physically push and pull two huge heavy gates required to close the fourteen-foot-high by eleven-foot-wide entrance. After I had made a drawing of the portcullis to the right scale, Mike assured me, after careful study, that he could produce it if he could examine some others. I gave him photographs, and also sent him off to Arundel Castle and one or two others which still had their original portcullises.'

About four months later the Bakers returned to find the portcullis installed, by which time the mechanism necessary to activate it was being shipped from America. To this day the porcullis is raised at seven o'clock every morning and lowered at midnight.

Because of the tourist traffic, particularly at weekends, the Bakers flew little red and white pennants from the northeast and northwest towers and a large St George's cross on a high flagstaff over the round towers at the entrance to indicate that the castle was inhabited. They also installed floodlights inside the courtyard, giving spectacular effects at night.

'There was one part of the courtyard to the west of the main entrance which was sealed by a ruined wall. This had been part of the barracks built for the Bishop's soldiers . . .The day came when I decided I could no longer stand this unattractive cul-de-sac and summoned the courage to have it cleaned out . . . This gave me a chance to clean out the small room west of the main entrance in the base of the tower. We placed an iron grille over the hole in the floor, which gave access to a circular pit some thirty feet deep . . .With the addition of the iron grille over the hole, it was easy to visualise this as a very unattractive prison. We enhanced the romance by slowly lowering a candle to the bottom for the benefit of visitors, and the effect was quite impressive.' The Bakers had discovered the oubliette.

Although they resisted the idea of opening the castle to the general public, they did conduct guided tours, with signs installed in strategic places to give a description of interesting parts of the ruins.

Mr and Mrs Peter Kirsh bought the castle in 1987. Although they were to stay for only a year, it proved an eventful time. The great storm which raged through southern England on the night of October 16, 1987 (known to all but meteorologists as 'the hurricane') ripped off the tiles over the east wing and brought down a huge mulberry tree that stood by the kitchen.

Another event during this year prefigured one of the popular uses of the castle today. 'My daughter was married in Amberley church,' Mr Kirsh recalls, 'and we had the wedding reception in the castle afterwards. It was a wonderful occasion in the perfect setting.'

Hollis MacLure Baker, the American owner in the early 1980s, reinstated Amberley's portcullis. It is raised (electrically) at 7 each morning and is lowered at midnight.

Amberley Wild Brooks

'Yearly the well-watered land produces a heavy crop of hay, and the horse-drawn waggons come lumbering with their scented loads day after day over the wild-brook meadows thro' a little lane whose . . . overhanging branches then trail a small hay-harvest of their own, across the railway track, and along under the old castle walls to the stackyards in the village.'

So wrote a local author in the *Sussex County Magazine* in 1939, reminding us of the agricultural importance of the dyke-drained pasture, scrub and woodland of the Wild Brooks, which for centuries provided local farmers with grazing and hay for their livestock. The name may be a corruption of Weald Brooks, for today's network of creeks originated in natural water-courses flowing southwards from the higher land above. In days gone by locals asked where they came from were said to exclaim

ABOVE Blue-tailed damselfly.

LEFT A painting from *Ornithological Rambles in Sussex*, by A.E. Knox, showing an osprey over the Wild Brooks with Amberley Castle in the middle distance. Knox, whose book was published in 1849, reported that ospreys had a great liking for the local grey mullet.

OPPOSITE PAGE TOP A view of the castle in 2001 with the Wild Brooks beyond.

RIGHT Pintail.

'from Amberley, thank God!' in high summer, but 'from Amberley, God help us!' in winter.

Today we value these 900 acres of wetland for their beauty and for the amazing variety of wildlife they contain. Indeed, the Wild Brooks played a leading role in the conservation debate in 1978, when naturalists sought to prevent a pump-drainage scheme which would have dried out the land for farmers, but at the cost of creating an ecological disaster. Two government bodies stood on either side of the divide, the Nature Conservancy Council (now English Nature) arguing for the preservation of one of the most

important wetland sites in lowland Britain, and the Ministry of Agriculture proposing to finance the drainage work.

'If the national interest is to be considered,' Dr David Streeter told the public enquiry, 'it is legitimate to argue that we should not be considering whether to spend large amounts of public money on improving the agricultural potential of low-grade farmland but to properly compensate the farmers in order to ensure the actual survival of high-grade conservation land.'

The argument in favour of leaving the wetlands untouched finally won the day, areas of nature reserve have been designated a Site of Special Scientific Interest and the Sussex Wildlife Trust now holds significant areas of the Wild Brooks, managed jointly with the Royal Society for the Protection of Birds. Their aim, here and in neighbouring tracts of the alluvial Arun Valley flooded plain such as Waltham Brooks and Pulborough Brooks, is to reverse the trend towards a drier, heavily-drained landscape – and already the numbers of wintering and breeding birds have begun to soar.

In summer, dragonflies, snails and water beetles flourish in the ditches, along with plants such as arrowhead and flowering rush. Grasshoppers chirp in the grasses, and butterflies flutter among the flowerheads. Birds of prey (hen harrier, merlin, buzzard, peregrine falcon, short-eared owl) stay here during the winter months, when there are also flocks of lapwing, teal, pochard and shoveler; Canada, grey lag and white-fronted geese; and mute and Bewick's swans. Come the spring, breeding lapwing, redshank, snipe and yellow wagtail perform their courtship displays over the tussocky marsh grasses and sedges.

'Here, if anywhere, one felt, the nature gods still stayed,' wrote the philosopher (and BBC radio Brains Trust star) C.E.M. Joad. 'this was one of their last lurking places.'

ABOVE The brooks are intersected by a network of ditches, rich in a diversity of wetland plant species.

OPPOSITE PAGE TOP large flocks of Bewick swans overwinter at the Wild Brooks.

RIGHT The Wild Brooks in flood.

Amberley Castle Today

ith tongues of fire shooting dramatically into the dark sky, local volunteer firemen rush to answer an emergency call to Amberley Castle. It is the evening of December 7, 1994, and the hotel chef has recoiled in incredulous horror to see the flames from his flambé sucked into an extractor fan. The kitchen is ablaze and the fire is spreading. Very soon there will be 15 tenders and 82 firemen at the scene.

The castle owners, Martin and Joy Cummings, receive the news on their mobile telephone while driving north for a family funeral. Fearing the worst, they immediately turn for home. Coming hard on the heels of a crippling recession which has ruined businesses up and down the land, this latest blow would be sufficient to break the spirit of lesser mortals – but the Cummings are made of sterner stuff.

Nothing better demonstrates the couple's determination and acumen than their swift response to this potentially devastating fire. It destroyed the kitchen, and four bedrooms were ruined by smoke and water damage, but within two days portable kitchens had been installed in the staff car park and the hotel was open for business again. Amberley Castle was about to enjoy its most glorious days since becoming (in the words of Marie Lloyd's music hall song) 'one of the ruins that Cromwell knocked about a bit' in the English Civil War.

'We needed to demonstrate that it had a future,' Martin Cummings explained afterwards. 'Pessimists might have expected us to throw in the towel. Indeed, some people might have suspected us of starting the fire ourselves – that wasn't unheard of in those difficult economic times – but we knew that Amberley Castle was a winner. Business had steadily improved ever since we opened it as a hotel.'

That was in 1988. The Cummings paid £2 million, and they were taking a risk. Not only was there no planning permission for its change

Martin and Joy Cummings with Oban and Amber and flanked by their children and grandchildren. Back row: daughter Andrea and her husband Dr Justin Kirk-Bayley; sons Oliver, Ross and Clive. Front Row: granddaughter Bethany, Martin & Joy, Lewis (grandson), Tanith (daughter-in-law, married to Clive) and Georgia (granddaughter).

Joy Cummings with the late Ronnie Maker, a much-loved Amberley villager who ceremoniously opened the castle as a country house hotel on July 29 1989.

RIGHT   Return of the fire fighters. Martin and Joy Cummings (seated), with the vicar and local villagers, welcome fire fighters from Storrington Fire Brigade to celebrate the restoration of the castle after the 1994 fire.
   It was members of the Storrington Fire Brigade who, together with the vicar Clive Jenkins, and villagers, assisted hotel residents to the Village Hall on the evening of the fire. Martin and Joy remain forever grateful for their help in a time of need.

of use to a hotel, but Horsham District Council had stipulated that it should remain as a private dwelling. Their bank lent them the money because of a highly impressive track record: they had turned round the fortunes first of the King's Arms Inn at Cookham-on-Thames, and then of The Inn on the Lake, near Goldalming in Surrey, an ailing business which had known five owners in five years (where they won two national hotel awards).

No sooner had they been granted permission to turn the castle into a luxury country house hotel, however, than the worst economic downturn since the Second World War set in. It was to be followed swiftly by the Gulf War and recession in America. British interest rates rose from 7½ per cent to 15 per cent and stayed at that level for a whole year. Worse still, the bank increased its margin from 2½ per cent to 3 per cent over base, so that the Cummings were faced with an overall rate of 18 per cent. Some £650,000 was needed for conversion costs, and a further £1.2 million of borrowing was added to the overdraft to cover interest rate payments. Every bill was settled on time – including

£3.5 million in interest payments over eight years – but it was impossible to repay a penny of capital.

Throughout this nightmare the Cummings still owned The Inn on the Lake. The plan had been to sell it as soon as Amberley Castle was purchased, but nobody wanted to make that kind of investment during a deepening recession. Home owners large and small were experiencing the pain of 'negative equity' as property prices collapsed – and so too the Cummings, but with 'noughts on'.

'At that stage the bank could have repossessed,' Martin Cummings reflected, 'but they didn't know what to do with a pile of stones in the middle of nowhere. They were stuck with Joy and me as the people who could make it work.'

Restoring and improving the gardens has been one of Martin Cummings' special projects over the years. This is one of the ponds, with its water lilies and koi carp.

Amberley Castle Costa

AMOROUS AMBERLEY

Several girls conceived in its historic rooms, or whose parents have been married within its walls, have been named after the castle – as the Cummings have learned from letters and photographs sent from all over the world.

The parents of Denise Amberley Nekeman in Holland, for instance, wrote enclosing a birthcard with little dragons on it: 'In a few years, when our daughter can really experience things, we plan to visit your hotel once more so that she can see that she has a little bit of royal blood. The little princess is sleeping in her room now.'

Sarah and Kostas Odysseas felt it only right to call their first daughter Amberley, following her birth a year and a day after their marriage at the castle in April 2001.

In California a couple with fond memories of their stay went one better. Each year they proudly send photographs of their daughter – Amberley Castle Costa.

The fire changed everything. At four o'clock the following morning Martin Cummings, swabbing out the charred remains of his kitchen, had answered the door to the insurance assessor. It was clear to this early-rising expert not only that the fire was, indeed, an accident, but that the hotel owners were set upon trading again very quickly. These were steely, battle-hardened winners. It was to be the bankers who lost their nerve.

Relationships between the Cummings and their Lloyds commercial bank manager had always been very good, indeed they had been with this bank for thirty-two years, but now the 'middle men' decided that they had had enough. They insisted on expensive insurance 'capping', additional management charges involving employing the management consultants Price Waterhouse (who duly recognised that this was a highly successful business, that the Cummings were 'performers' and that the hotel's accounts were exemplary), together with a range of other financial impositions. The Cummings were hauled before the bank's solicitors in London and given what they regarded as a hostile and demeaning dressing-down. They were instructed to sell the castle.

Serious battle now commenced, with Martin Cummings writing a detailed, impassioned backs-to-the-wall letter, dated June 24, 1997, to the bank's chairman, Sir Brian Pitman. Protesting about the bank's decision to cut and run, he pointed out that the Cummings (in danger of losing their home as well as their business) had met every interest payment without delay or demand. Turnover had mushroomed, interest rate-only payments had been achieved since 1991-2 and business was currently 20 per cent higher than the year before.

This adroit letter won a stay of execution, but the vital relationship between bank and client had been soured for ever.

'I'm afraid that it had gone steadily from bad to worse,' Martin Cummings said later, 'while the castle itself had gone from strength to strength. We'd worked every hour there was to save it, couples flocked to stay in it from all over the world and all we got was shabby treatment in return.'

'And sleepless nights,' recalled Joy Cummings. 'Many of those, for me at least. We could imagine ourselves homeless despite everything that we had achieved.'

When Barclays Bank offered a better deal the Cummings accepted without a second thought – and the soundness of its judgement is

The surroundings are special, but so is the food: Amberley Castle has won several prestigious awards for its cuisine.

evident in the cluster of prestigious awards Amberley Castle proceeded to gain for its accommodation and its cuisine. Notable among these was being voted into 'the world's top 20 leisure hotels' by readers of Condé Nast *Traveller* magazine for two consecutive years, 2000 and 2001.

The Cummings 'secret' was to plough all their profits back into the business, improving the castle's facilities year by year, and carefully harnessing their talents: Martin (from Northumberland, like the great St Wilfrid) learnt his management skills at the John Lewis Partnership

HMS *Amberley Castle*

On a wall in the castle near the restaurant is a photograph of Her Majesty's Ship *Amberley Castle*, one of 24 anti-submarine corvettes commiss-ioned during the Second World War.

The photograph was a gift from Keith McKenna of Footprints, and a singularly fitting one – Martin Cummings served in the Royal Navy for twelve years from a boy, and he was born in 1943, the year in which HMS *Amberley Castle* was launched.

With a displacement of just over 1,000 tons these 'Castle Class' ships had a rated sea speed of over 16 knots – about 20 mph. HMS *Amberley Castle* was fully fitted-out for warfare in 1944. She carried a crew of 96, was fitted with two 40mm anti-aircraft guns and two smaller 20mm guns, and had a 'Squid' three-barrelled anti-ship mortar. She also carried 15 depth charges, which could be despatched from two rear launchers. Postwar she was reclassified as a frigate.

The only other Sussex name selected for one of these ships was HMS *Bramber Castle*, but the order for her was cancelled at the end of the war and she was never built.

Today there are just two of these vessels left in service: HMS *Leeds Castle* and HMS *Dumbarton Castle*, operating as offshore patrol vessels for the Fisheries Protection Squadron.

(Waitrose), while Joy trained in catering. They also had no doubts they had chosen the right place from the evening when, having read in *Country Life* magazine that the castle was on the market, they drove down unannounced from Surrey to see whether it matched their requirements.

'The one thing you're looking for in a country house hotel is uniqueness,' Martin Cummings explained. 'You need to have something that the other guy hasn't got. When we found our way down in the dark, it was closed up and all we could see was rabbits running all over the place. We came up the drive and put the car headlights on – and then we saw the walls. They make the place unique, and not only in this country: it's possibly the only hotel in the whole world which is inside a medieval castle with 60ft curtain walls.'

Between 1988 and 2003 – the castle's 900th anniversary year – the improvements continued apace. Joy Cummings has overseen a steady refurbishment of the interior, upgrading rooms already full of character and history by giving them new bathrooms and four-poster beds, replacing the reproduction furniture with antiques and so on – putting, as she says, 'the icing on the cake'.

Martin Cummings, a keen gardener, has not only continued Baroness Emmet's work within the walls but has transformed the exterior grounds, too. The two large fields in front of the castle have been landscaped, with four small lakes, while the size of the ornamental gardens has been doubled, and a tennis court and an eighteen-hole

professional putting green have been introduced in addition to the croquet lawn.

Two stone seventeenth century buildings within the dry moat have been transformed into five suites and a further two will be converted from the Emmets' former stables. The cellars are earmarked for a sauna, solarium and steam room, while the Water Gate garden will have a fountain and rills. The Duke of Norfolk, as we have seen, repaired some of the crenellations, and the Cummings hope one day to restore more of them at the front of the castle.

At weekends the castle is always fully booked, with about three-quarters of the guests British, 17 per cent American (rising to 35 per cent in the summer), five per cent Europeans and the rest coming from around the world, particularly Japan and Australia. During the week, especially in the winter months, companies book rooms for meetings,

ABOVE LEFT Each bedroom at Amberley Castle has its own special character. This is the Arundel bedroom, which like many of the guest bedrooms includes a four-poster bed.

ABOVE Martin Cummings busy in his garden – where he prefers to be!

AGMs, 'product launches', parties and special events. Martin Cummings, who himself flies a helicopter, is delighted to invite fellow pilots literally to drop in for these and other occasions.

Perhaps the biggest growth has been in weddings. (Two of the Cummings' four children, Clive and Andrea, had their receptions here after being married in Amberley church.) Several rooms in the castle are licensed for the civil marriage service, and hundreds of couples tie the knot here every year – some, very occasionally, choosing to visit alone, with the staff as witnesses to their very special day, but many booking the whole castle for an unforgettable house party.

'We may have had the vision to create a hotel in a castle,' says Martin Cummings, 'but our customers take the prize when it comes to how best

ABOVE   Ever improving: the Bishopric suites outside the castle walls.

RIGHT   The castle is the ultimate romantic setting for a wedding – the happy couple in this case being Andrea, the Cummings' daughter, and Dr Justin Kirk-Bayley.

ON BENDED KNEE

The romantic atmosphere at Amberley Castle has encouraged many a suitor to propose here, occasionally in extravagant fashion. Rings have been inserted in puddings, a lavish firework display has proved an irresistible prelude to popping the question, while one ardent lover dressed himself in a suit of armour and cantered under the portcullis on a white charger.

to use it. Castles are places of imagination and dreams. When the portcullis is lowered at night the walls create a sense of total quiet and seclusion. We like to think that more people are enjoying Amberley Castle today than ever before in its long history.

'From day one the castle has been a real gem. Through thick and thin, it has never let us down.'

Businessmen sometimes fly in to Amberley Castle for conferences and other events by helicopter.

Amberley Village
'The Pearl of Sussex'

One of the delights of stepping out from Amberley Castle is exploring the little village which has grown outside its walls. Amberley, known as 'the pearl of Sussex', is simplicity itself. Its unpretentious but beautifully kept cottages occupy a quadrilateral of lanes, one of them extending as a cul-de-sac towards the church and the castle. As all villages should, it has a village shop, a pond and a couple of pubs (the Black Horse near the centre and the Sportsman half-a-mile away.) The downs rise in front to the south, while the Wild Brooks lie below to the north, fringed by the hills of the weald. The feeling is of a timeless scene, although the very names of the cottages – the Bakery, the Malt House, the Brew House and so on – hint at activities which have long since disappeared.

The author Arthur Mee described Amberley as 'one of the gems of the loveliest countryside on earth, with a river flowing through its green

ABOVE Horses drinking in the village pond in about 1880, with Rock Cottage, St Michael's Church, and the castle behind.

BELOW Haymaking at Amberley in about 1910.

meadows, thatched houses in its lanes, a feast of beauty in its church and a stirring of history in its ancient castle walls.'

More down to earth, the topographical author Ian Nairn called it one of the show villages of Sussex, enthusing about its 'anthology of building materials – thatch and tile, brick, flint, half-timber, and Burgate stone, and also just a little clunch.'

Even the name (the 'ley' part means meadow) feels just right. In his book *The South Country* the poet and topographical author Edward Thomas, writes about the many alluring village names of southern England. 'I once tried to make a beautiful name,' he reveals, 'and in the end it was Amberley, in which Time had forestalled me'.

Some of the buildings have stones quarried from the castle visible in their structure – notably Rock Cottage, hard by the castle walls, which is now the home of the Cummings' son Clive (manager of the hotel), his wife Tanith and their children. Another is Amberley House, built on the site of three old cottages by an American, Alfred Parrish, in 1911.

Artists, not surprisingly, have flocked to Amberley over the years with their easels – to such an extent that the village schoolmaster once complained of a regrettable absenteeism because so many of the children were being employed as models. One who lived here (in what is now Stott's Corner) was Edward Stott, who first made his reputation at the close of the 19th century and who is remembered in

Rock Cottage, built in the shadow of the castle wall, is now the home of the hotel manager Clive Cummings, his wife Tanith and their children.

The cottages in Amberley village are immensely varied in style and in the materials used to build them.

ABOVE Oak Tree Cottage.

RIGHT Church Street, with the Studio in the foreground and the Bakery beyond.

a stained glass window in St Michael's Church.

Fishermen once came here in vast numbers, too. In that bible of the sport, *The Compleat Angler*, Isaak Walton writes that 'Sussex boast(s) of several fish; as namely, a Selsey cockle, a Chichester lobster, an Arundel mullet and an Amerly trout.' In Victorian times swarms of south Londoners would descend upon the village on Sundays during the season to enjoy coarse fishing in

the Arun: in October 1891, for instance, two special trains brought 300 competitors and more than 800 other fishermen and supporters. The contestants were so keen that they would arrive the day before fishing was due to begin, setting off at midnight to secure the best positions by the water.

Quieter today, the village continues to attract visitors in search of a rare beauty and tranquillity.

'It has retained the charm of age but has banished the squalor,' observes that fine Sussex writer Ben Darby.

'Thatched roofs crown flint, timber-framed and whitewashed walls, and the whole immaculate village suggests an attitude of disdain for the vulgarity and noise of the twentieth century without sinking to the silliness of "ye olde". It has been preserved but not mummified.'

Amberley Timeline

St Wilfrid granted land by the king, in about 680 AD

1066 William I, the Conqueror

1087 William II, Rufus
    1091-1123 Bishop Ralph Luffa

    1100 Henry I
    c. 1103 Luffa builds hunting lodge at Amberley
    1108 Formal dedication of Chichester cathedral
    1114 Fire badly damages cathedral
1124-47 Bishop Seffrid I

1135 Stephen
    c. 1140 Seffrid I builds first stone hall at Amberley
    1180-1204 Bishop Seffrid II
    1184 Repaired cathedral re-consecrated under Seffrid II
    1187 Another fire guts cathedral and bishop's palace

1154 Henry III

1189 Richard, the Lionheart

1199 John
    1199 Cathedral re-consecrated for second time
    c1200 Seffrid II builds Amberley's east wing

1216 Henry III
    1224-45 Bishop Ralph Neville rebuilds chancel of Amberley parish church
    1245-46 Disputed consecration of Richard de Wych (declared a saint 1262)

1272 Edward I
    1292 Richard FitzAlan excommunicated for hunting at Houghton
    1305-37 Bishop John of Langton builds Great Hall at Amberley Castle

1307 Edward II

1327 Edward III
    1349 Black Death arrives in Sussex; at least a third of the population dies

1377 Richard II

    1370-1385 Bishop Reede builds new Great Hall; makes major domestic improvements
    1377 Bishop Reede given permission to crenellate Amberley Castle
    1381 Peasants' Revolt

1399 Henry IV

1413 Henry V
    1415 Earliest reference to a prison at Amberley Castle

1422 Henry VI
    1450 Jack Cade's rebellion
    c.1450 Stone bridge built across the Arun at Houghton
    1449 Bishop Adam Moleyns assassinated by sailors

1461 Edward IV

1483 Richard III

1485 Henry VII
    1508-36 Bishop Sherborne embellishes Amberley Castle; employs Lambert Bernard as court painter.

1509 Henry VIII
    c.1525 Lambert Bernard paints Amberley Panels
    1526 Henry VIII visits Bishop Sherborne
    1536-40 Dissolution of the monasteries
    1538 Church leases Amberley Castle to tenant for first time

1547 Edward VI

1553 Mary, 'Bloody'

1558 Elizabeth I
    1588 Spanish Armada
    1588 Amberley Castle leased to the Crown

1603 James I

1624 Charles I

    1642 Civil War breaks out
    1644 Amberley's defences dismantled by Waller's troops
    1648 James Butler buys Amberley from commissioners of sequestered estates
    1649 Charles I beheaded
    1651 Flight of the future Charles II through Sussex

1649 Commonwealth (Cromwell)

1660 Charles II
    1660 Estate reverts to bishopric
    1661 Butlers acquires lease
    1683 Sir John Briscoe acquires lease: hunting scene painted in Queens' Room

1685 James II

1688 William & Mary

1702 Anne

1714 George I

1727 George II

1737 Engraving of the castle by Samuel and Nathaniel Buck

1760 George III
    1788 Grimm drawings of the castle

1820 George IV
    1820 Grieg engraving

1830 William IV

1837 Victoria
    1893 Duke of Norfolk purchases Amberley Castle, ending ecclesiastical ownership

1901 Edward VII
    1908 Duke of Norfolk makes repairs at Amberley

1910 George V
    1920 Walter Peckham visits Amberley and draws ground plan
    1925 Thomas and Evelyn Emmet purchase Amberley Castle
    1925 Second Peckham visit

1936 Edward VIII (abdicates)

1936 George VI
    1945 Princess Elizabeth visits the castle

1952 Elizabeth II
    1982 Hollis Baker purchases
    1987 Peter Kirsh purchases
    1988 Martin and Joy Cummings purchase the castle

Acknowledgements

An enormous number of people have helped make this book possible, and I am grateful to all of those who have played a part in its creation. My first and greatest debt is to Martin and Joy Cummings, the driving force behind its production, and without whom it would never have become a reality. The book's high quality owes much to their generosity, and to their determination to mark the 900th anniversary of the castle's initial construction in a style worthy of its remarkable history.

I am particularly grateful to Dr Annabelle Hughes, on whose research I have drawn heavily for much of the text: in a sense I am reaping the harvest she sowed. A special debt is owed to Eugene Roberts, responsible for Amberley Castle's Public Relations, who has overseen the production on Martin Cummings behalf: no obstacle has defeated her, no request met with anything other than unflappable calmness and efficiency.

I am also grateful to Ann Money-Coutts and Lavinia Fleming for so generously providing the Emmet family photographs that appear between pages 77 and 81. I would also like to thank Ann Smith for the English translation of the 'licence to crenellate' on page 30. Keith McKenna was most helpful with information about HMS *Amberley Castle* and provided the photograph of the vessel on page 96.

On behalf of the publishers and Martin and Joy Cummings, I would like to thank the following for providing illustrations, or for allowing the inclusion of illustrations in their possession or for which they hold the copyright: Amberley Working Museum, page 42 (top); David Brindley, pages 13, 15, 16, 46, 51; by permission of the British Library (ADD. MSS 5674, f6 drawings 10/11, f7, drawings 12/13), pages 64 (bottom), 65, 66, 67; Christopher Chaplin, pages 18 (top), 26, 30; Geoff Childs, pages 81 (left), 98 (left); the Costa family, page 94; Mark Dennis Photography, pages 95 (left), 96 (left); John Hodgson for his marvellous reconstruction of the medieval castle on pages 32/33 and the oubliette on page 35; Jarrold Photography (photograph by Peter Smith), page 47; Iain McGowan, pages 40/41 (top), 41 (bottom), 43, 72/73, 89 (bottom), 102, 103; by kind permission of His Grace The Duke of Norfolk, pages 71, 75; Mike Read, pages 12, 17, 40 (bottom left), 42 (top and bottom left), 86 (right), 87 (bottom), 88, 89 (top); Robert Soudain, pages 14, 34, 39, 57, 59, 61 (left); Split Image, front and back cover, the frontispiece photograph on pages 2/3, 8, 10, 20 (left), 21, 23, 26, 27, 28, 35, 45 (both), 62, 83, 90, 95, 101; Venture Portraits, pages 4, 6, 44, 50, 53, 54, 55, 56, 63, 74, 85, 92 (both), 93, 97 (right), 98 (right), 99; West Sussex Record Office, pages 68 (top), 82 (this photograph is part of the Garland Collection held by West Sussex Record Office).

All the remaining illustrations come from the collections of the author, Martin and Joy Cummings, and The Dovecote Press Ltd.

Index

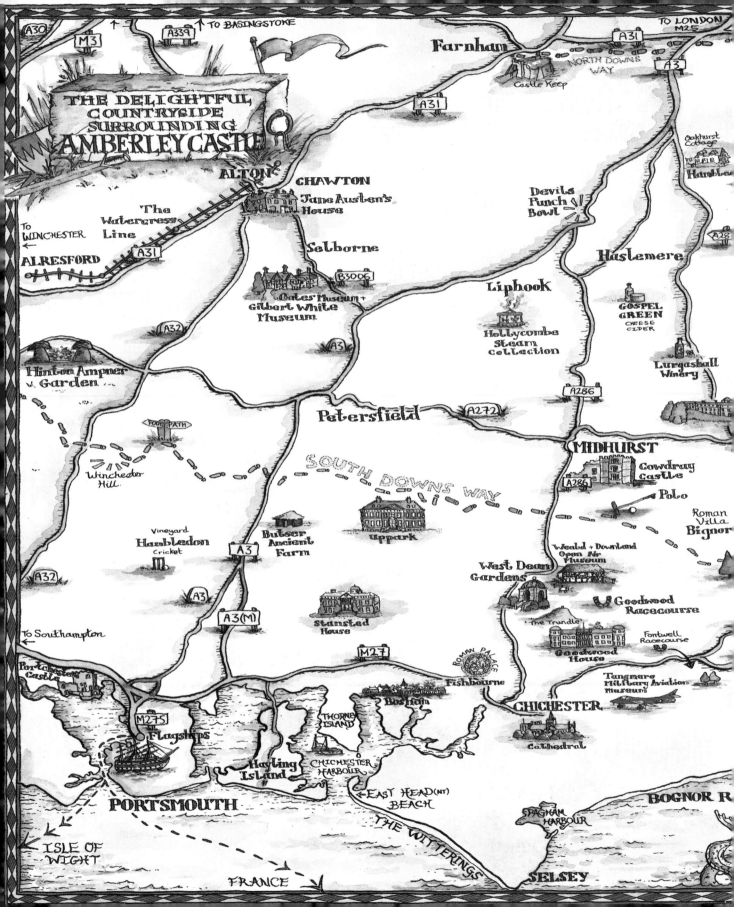